RAW CHOCTAW

Memoirs of an Indian Medicine Woman

By Lady Nellie M. Thompson

With Wendy Cope

authorHOUSE®

AuthorHouse™
1663 Liberty Drive, Suite 200
Bloomington, IN 47403
www.authorhouse.com
Phone: 1-800-839-8640

© 2010 Lady Nellie M. Thompson with Wendy Ann Cope. All rights reserved.

No part of this book may be reproduced, stored in a retrieval system, or transmitted by any means without the written permission of the author.

First published by AuthorHouse 2/8/2010

ISBN: 978-1-4490-5529-5 (e)
ISBN: 978-1-4490-5528-8 (sc)
ISBN: 978-1-4490-5530-1 (hc)

Library of Congress Control Number: 2009912811

Printed in the United States of America
Bloomington, Indiana

This book is printed on acid-free paper.

Edited by: Richard Peterson

Forward from Chief Gregory E. Pyle
Choctaw Tribal Leader of the Choctaw Nation

The Choctaws were the first of the tribes to be removed on the "Trail of Tears" to Indian Territory, later Oklahoma. After signing the Treaty of Dancing Rabbit Creek September 30, 1830, the Choctaws began to get ready to leave Mississippi for their new home. Although more tribes followed on similar journeys in a long, sad march, the Choctaws coined the phrase "Trail of Tears".

Southeastern Oklahoma continues to be the Choctaw Nation tribal boundaries, and a separate tribe, the Mississippi Band of Choctaws, is made up of descendants from the Choctaws who chose to remain in the ancestral homeland rather than travel to the new Nation in Indian Territory. The Choctaw Nation of Oklahoma operates with a three branch democratic government, Executive, Legislative and Judicial. There are close to 200,000 tribal members worldwide.

The Choctaw Nation provides many services to tribal members and also assists communities, churches and public offices. In addition to the 5,000 scholarships given annually, the tribe administrates education programs such as Head Start, Adult Education, Vocational Development, Jones Academy residential school and Choctaw Language classes.

Comprehensive health care is provided to Choctaws at a hospital in Talihina and clinics in Stigler, Poteau, Broken Bow, Idabel, McAlester, Hugo and Atoka. There is also a Diabetes Center and wellness centers in the Choctaw Nation. Many social services for Choctaws of all ages are available.

Heritage is very important to the Choctaw Nation, and we celebrate the past, present and future in activities that are open to the public. Each year, there is a Commemorative Trail of Tears Walk, Labor Day Festival, and Veterans Ceremony. Sharing history through stories, whether oral or written, is an important work. I thank Lady Nellie for sharing her personal memories with the rest of us.

Chief Gregory E. Pyle

Choctaw Nation of Oklahoma

This book is dedicated to my beloved Choctaw Tribe, my loving family, and to Jesus—all a great part of my life.

Wendy, my dear little angel, the most beautiful person in the world I feel like, and the most helpful—she has just really helped me through this thing. It sure makes me happy. I'm grateful to have her as a friend, and if it come down to it, I would even smoke the peace pipe with her. I want to thank her for this blessing, and each and every one of you that is reading my story.

Introduction

Nellie Morse Thompson had never learned to read or write. That's what I learned the first time we met that sunny afternoon in June 2006. We sat in patio chairs in the backyard of a mutual friend and talked in the shade of a large canvas umbrella.

"I went to school for forty days," Nellie said, tapping her red polished fingernails against the knees of her cotton pants. "My school teacher—her name was Mrs. McGraw—told me, 'You're sick, honey, you're sick.' She put her hand on my forehead and said, 'Your head is so hot I can't hold my hand on it. You're going to have to go home.'

"I had Malero Fever. Now days, they call it Rheumatic Fever. That was the last day of the forty days that I spent in school. Since then, one thing I always wanted to do was go to school and get an education and be as smart as other people."

As I listened, I was intrigued by Nellie. Here she was, eighty-eight years old—a lot older than most people, and wanted to learn to read. I decided I wanted to teach her because, after all, I was trained in literacy instruction.

And this is how it all began.

Two weeks later, I found myself sitting in her Modesto, California, home, teaching her to read and write. I'll never forget arriving for our first lesson. I parked my car in front of her house. Through the woven slats in the fence I noticed a lemon tree shading a small area of patchy grass and two brown cement lion statues, facing one another, as if to guard the gated entrance; I stared at the sand-colored stucco siding, the arch above the entryway.

I walked along the cracked cement path leading to her home and was greeted by the sweet smell of roses and the sight of knickknacks on display —pots, vases, an assortment of statues, small wooden carvings anchored to metal stakes driven in the ground. Off to my right, under a large sugar pine tree, were two tables filled with black, green, gold, and clear glass-like rocks that glittered in the sunlight.

I tapped on a metal screen and stared at a pink carpet piece under my feet until the door swung open and on the other side, Nellie's daughter Leona appeared. As Leona and I gazed at each other, I heard Nellie's voice. "Hello, darling, come in. I've been waiting for you." From her chair she held her arms out to me with a huge grin painted on her face. We hugged as if we were old friends, and I settled into a chair next to her and sighed from the weariness of the long, two-hour drive.

I looked around. Her house was packed with things. One entire wall was filled with shelves, housing collections of trinkets—there were a hundred or more, some made of porcelain, others glass. Another wall was decorated with plaques and awards. I strained my eyes and read the words on one: Nellie Thompson, In Appreciation for Years of Service to the Veterans.

There were lots of pictures of Jesus around; Mary with Jesus, The Last Supper, Jesus on the cross.

I looked at Nellie, at her remarkably smooth skin, at her curls of hair fluttering in a stream of air blowing from the swamp cooler. Then my eyes wandered past her to a picture that hung in the window sill, of an Indian man on a dream-catcher. Large brown feathers dangled from the picture's wooden frame.

We spent most of our time that day sounding out alphabet letters. She remembered Mrs. McGraw teaching her sounds, but eighty years later the actual sounds had mostly faded from her memory. I showed her where to place her tongue to sound out the *R*s and the *L*s, and when we got to the letter *X* she made a scratchy noise that sounded as though she were clearing her throat. It made us both laugh.

I came back the following Tuesday and brought several stacks of word flash cards and a pad of paper. We reviewed sounds and practiced writing alphabet letters. She wrote her name across a piece of paper in shaky cursive letters: Nellie Thompson.

She told me more about her family. She said her "papa" had worked as a surveyor for the Choctaw Lumber Company, hauling logs and railroad ties.

"What's a railroad tie?" I asked.

"Oh, it's something that helps hold the tracks together," she explained.

What? I don't understand.

She used a piece of paper and began drawing a picture.

"A railroad tie helps support the train," she said, pointing to her picture.

I shifted the paper around to see what she was drawing, but it still didn't make sense to me.

I'll just Google it, I told her.

"Huh?" she said, confused. "What's a Google?"

We paused, looked at each other for a moment then burst out laughing again. Laughing together was something we would do often as we became better acquainted.

The following Tuesday we read together, practiced writing, and spent more time talking about her life. On my way home I realized that what she was telling me was so interesting I wanted to have her tape her story so I could transcribe it. I called her right then, and we talked about the possibility.

"Oh, Wendy, I'd be delighted!" she said. "I've been waiting for the right person, and that's you!"

In the following months our tutoring lessons took a lesser priority as our real project unfolded. Nellie began sharing her memories, and I began organizing the information.

As I transcribed her story, a problem became apparent. Although Nellie's recollections are extraordinarily detailed, she was understandably unable to accurately recall certain dates and locations. This made the stories incomplete and somewhat incomprehensible. Additionally, moves and extenuating circumstances led to the misplacing of many of the family's documents.

In effort to create an accurate history of Nellie's life, I spent many days researching. I found great success at the LDS Church History Library in Salt Lake City, Utah. With the help of several Native American expert researchers and other helpful staff members, many fascinating discoveries were found in Nellie's life, which you will find throughout this book.

Over the course of eighteen months, Nellie and I have teamed together to capture her story—by way of tape recordings, many telephone conversations, frequent personal meetings, and by travels together to Oklahoma, Arkansas, and Texas, places where Nellie relived many of the stories recorded in this account. One of the highlights of our travels, and the fulfillment of a dream of Nellie's, was meeting with Chief Gregory E. Pyle, Choctaw Tribal Leader of the Choctaw Nation, in May 2007.

The result of our efforts is this inspiring, true account of a Choctaw Indian woman's life, whose courage and faith in God have moved her through many difficult trials. Woven into her stories is a fresh, first-hand perspective of a history and culture that would otherwise be lost. I hope you enjoy getting to know this charming and remarkable woman as much as I have.

Chapter One
1918

It was straight up twelve o'clock midnight, according to Grandmother, and I was born a princess by the signs of the moon. Grandpa Williams put a blanket over his hands and left me uncovered and walked outside the teepee and held me up to the light of the moon. He offered blessings to the Great White Father and declared me a princess.

It scared Grandma. She was afraid I'd get sick out there in the cold. She called out, "John T., you're gonna kill that child! The night air is cold and that child is bare."

"This child is a princess and she must be strong," Grandpa said. "She will live a long life and will have to endure many things."

With tears in his eyes, Grandpa lowered me from the light of the moon and brought me back into the arms of my mother.

I was born Nellie Morse, to Fred J. and Nannie Chandler Williams Morse, February the 21, 1918, on a reservation in Tom, Oklahoma. I've always said I was born in 1912, but there are other readings that say different. When I was in an orphanage they changed the date on me. Since we've been writing this book we've found other reasons to believe that I was born in 1918, or right along in there.

My first home on the reservation was cozy. There was a fire in the middle of the teepee, and the smoke would go out of the hole in the top. Once in a while, the wind changed and let the smoke back in. Then we had to open the flap and let the smoke out. The beds were up on wooden stilts and made out of hay. Most all the bedding was either crocheted out of wool thread or made out of buckskin—the hide off a male deer.

One night, I was sleeping in the teepee, and I awoke with my left leg crampin' so bad I was crying. My grandfather got up with me and rubbed my legs. He said he couldn't see nothin' wrong with them, but they were still drawing double. I couldn't even stand on them. In the following weeks, the doctor pronounced me with polio. I was three years old at that time. To start out with, it got in my left side, and I couldn't hold nothin' in my left hand. If I held a glass of water, it would turn lose and fall out of my hand. My daddy ordered me a tin cup with a handle on it so's I could hold onto it while I drink my milk or water. If I did drop it, it wouldn't break.

Then the polio finally covered my whole body.

I was stiff and I couldn't move hand nor foot until someone would come and move me. Whatever way I was when I went to sleep, that is the way I would stay all night. I would have nights that I'd have to force myself to move one leg or the other—it's usually my right leg that still to this day is a little stiff.

Papa made me a little cane-bottom chair 'cause I could no longer stand on my own two feet. I was bound to that little chair. If I got in it, I couldn't get out of it. I had to be toted around like a little baby, and it was certainly embarrassing. If anyone mentioned me not being able to walk, I'd break down in tears. I'd tell them, "I didn't do this on purpose."

On the reservation we farmed corn, sweet potatoes, peanuts, tomatoes, and turnips and greens. Mama showed me how to shell the corn. Papa would break the corn off the stalks and bring them to the teepee. We left the shuck on the cob over the fire until the corn was roasted and good and brown and then we would take the corn and lay them off the fire until they cooled down for us to shuck. We would take one piece of the shuck and lay it back and sprinkle a little salt, a little sugar, and a little butter, and then wrap it back up until it cooled down. And, oh, boy! That was the best corn you ever tasted. Mama made everything out of corn. She made cornbread, mush, fried tortillas, corn muffins, and hominy.

We lived on the Indian reservation, and Papa was a farmin' and everything was going along alright, but then Oklahoma took all the Indians' money; took every dime they had. Closed down the banks—went bankrupt, I guess. I remember Papa said, "We can't make it here on the farm. We'll have to leave here and go to the mountains, and I'll get me a job working as a surveyor for the Choctaw Lumber Company."

I was four years old when we left the Indian reservation, my sister Hattie was seven years old, and my baby sister, Edny, was but eighteen months. We loaded up everything we had that we could take on our wagon. It was Mama and us girls, and Papa and Uncle Clarence, Mama's baby brother. Uncle Clarence was a tall, broad-shouldered Indian boy with coal-black hair, dark brown eyes, and the prettiest smile. During that time all the men folks went off to the war to fight the battle, but they didn't draft Clarence 'cause he wasn't old enough.

There were girls anywhere from twelve to eighteen years old on the reservation that claimed him for their boyfriend. He was well-loved by all the girls, and he would always give them a helping hand. If they was in the wagon he would lift them down, or if they were cuttin' or carrying wood he would always do that for them, too. He'd also help hang their clothes on the line. I heard him tell Papa when we got up into the mountains, "I sure miss the girls, Uncle Fred. I sure miss the girls on the reservation."

When we first begin to pack up, we put the food basket at the very back end of the wagon so's we could get to it while we were traveling. Papa covered all our belongings with a tarp and then took ropes and tied everything down so our things wouldn't shake and fall off the wagon.

Papa handed me to Uncle Clarence, and Uncle Clarence turned around and set me in Mama's rocking chair on top of everything in the wagon. I felt like I was the most special one of the whole bunch. They always took good care of me. It was always, "Do this for Nellie, and do that for Nellie." Uncle Clarence set up there by me on the bed covers, and Papa, Mama, Hattie, and Edna rode down on the front of the wagon on the springseat. Mama held Edny because she would feed her with the breast while we went along.

Mama made blankets for us to wrap up in. She made our blankets off the scraps of our dresses. Mine was rather special. It was made out of the pattern called the Little Dutch Girl; Hattie's quilt pattern was a little smoothing iron, and Edny's little blanket was out of the spotted hound dog because she liked the dog so well.

Papa hooked the two horses we had to the wagon. One of them was a glaze-face with a snow-white strip between her ears and down to her nose. She was a beautiful horse. The other one was plain red, but smooth and slick and had a long mane. Papa would click his tongue so the horses would get up and shake the lines so they would start walking fast. Papa would never whip a horse. He was one of the men that was always kind and loved his horses.

We were getting ready to pull out for the beautiful Kiamichi Mountains, and Mama looked all sad and broke up. Papa took her in his arms and hugged and kissed her. "Everything is going to be alright. Now don't you worry, darling, me and Clarence almost have the cabin built, and it won't take long to finish it once we get there."

After Papa and Uncle Clarence built the cabin, they came down out of the mountains to get Mama an' us kids.

We said goodbye to one another, and our friends waved at us as far as they could see us. I was crying, Mama was a crying, and Hattie and Edny was a crying. We were all crying because we had to leave the Indian reservation.

I was gonna miss all the people that loved us so much. We were a big family, and it was breakin' our hearts to part from each other. As I was leaving the reservation I remembered the good times. I remembered playing Ring-around-the-Rosie with all the other girls. They would take me and set me in the chair, and we'd gather up and make a ring holding hands. We would start out singing:

Ring around the Rosie,
Pocket full of posies,
The last one squats
On an old grey hen!

I remembered the wolves howling at night and the moon a shinin' so bright you could see shadows on the ground. I remembered everyone gather'n' together around the fire, dancing and laughing and hollering and doing the pow-wow. I was leaving all of our friends of every kind and color. I was so sad. I listened to the sound of the howling of the wolves and the Indians' pow-wows and everything stood still.

As we were headed for the mountains, the beautiful Kiamichi Mountains, the fields were all green, and the birds were flying—the doves and the quail and, occasionally, a crow or two. The road was rough and bumpy. If you've ever been on a dirt road in Oklahoma, you know what I'm talking about. They were winding and had deep curves and were beat out in places. It was awfully rough goin'.

My sister Hattie would get up close to me where I was sitting in Mother's rocking chair, and we would play Tic-Tac-Toe on our slate board. We had to entertain ourselves for a long time. Mama would sing, and whenevern' she would sing, the wagon wheels would squeak and make a beautiful sound that blended right in with her melodies. As we would move along, her voice would expand clear across the country. It was like the whole universe was enjoying her. Even the trees and the wind enjoyed her melody. The time would pass by faster, the wheels would roll faster, and the birds and the fowl appeared to sing along with her. Mama's favorite song was, "When the Roll Is Called up Yonder, I'll Be There."

Let us labor for the Master from the dawn till setting sun,
Let us talk of all His wondrous love and care;
Then when all of life is over, and our work on earth is done,
And the roll is called up yonder, I'll be there.

After she would sing, everything got still and quiet.

I think we was three days on the road—from sun up 'til sundown. When dusk of dark come that first day, we found a place to camp near the Kiamichi River. The camp place that Papa picked was beautiful. It was down close to the river, and it was quiet, other than the whistling of the birds. The sky was a clear blue with a haze comin' over it just as the sun was drawing down. It was the most beautiful sight I ever seen.

From my chair, I watched everything take place. Papa prepared a place for us to sleep, Hattie helped unload the wagon, and Uncle Clarence and Mama cleared a small area of brushwood, so there was no danger of fire. Later in the evening, we would build a fire, Mother would cook, and Papa and Uncle Clarence let the horses go to get something to eat.

Chapter Notes

Kiamichi Mountains: A heavily mountainous and forested region of southeastern Oklahoma.

Tom, Oklahoma: Tom is a small unincorporated community in McCurtain County, Oklahoma, United States. The post office was established in 1916 and named for Tom Stewart, an early settler. It is the southeasternmost community in Oklahoma.

The war that was mentioned was World War I, fought from 1914-1918.

Chapter Two
1922

Papa and Uncle Clarence went hunting and for supper brought in two rabbits, a coon, and a bundle of snakeroot. Uncle Clarence held the legs of the rabbits, while Papa skinned them and got them ready for cookin'. Mama would later clean and tan the skins to make moccasins out of. They never wasted nothin'. One raccoon skin usually made several caps, and the one that got the raccoon tail to hang down his back would put the cap on and dance around the fire in celebration.

Papa would take some forked limbs and lay a pole across it and tie the coon and rabbits on the pole over the hot coals to cook. Mama would rub the meat down with salt and pepper and then tie the animal's legs together on this pole so they could turn them over the fire and cook them nice and brown. While Mama was cooking, Papa was boiling up snakeroot tea to keep us from getting malaria fever from the mosquitoes.

Mama made what we call pancakes now, but she called them hoecakes back then. We ate the hoecakes and the meat from the rabbits and the coon. Uncle Clarence made the comment that there was nothing better to eat than the hare and the hoes. Everybody laughed at Uncle Clarence 'cause he was what they called a comedian. He was always making jokes about something or someone. I loved it because his big old brown eyes would light up when he would tell something funny.

While we were eating, there was a pair of big, dark eyes that appeared out in the woods. We were all scared. Us three girls huddled up around Mama until Papa could see what it was. Papa gets the gun and goes off into the woods to see if he could tell what it was. It was a deer. Papa said, "We will be seeing a lot of those up in the mountains and around. We need not to be scared."

Mama laid out two blankets on the ground that was made of buffalo hide and built our sleeping pallets on them. Papa took a grubbing hoe and dug a little ditch around the buffalo hide 'cause that would keep the snakes from gettin' in bed with us. We all slept on the buffalo hide inside of the circle. Me, Hattie, and Edny, cuddled up real close to stay warm and to stay safe. Out in the bushes and away from the campfire, every once in awhile, you would see two eyes—sometimes four eyes. It was two heads of coyote or two deer. I felt scared and uneasy and would hold my sisters close while we slept.

Two days later we arrived at the log cabin. I stared up at the trees. There was nothing but trees—just as far as the eye could see. They surrounded the cabin and went on miles and miles over the mountains and down in the valleys. It was such a beautiful scene of nature to stand and look out over that ocean of trees. As I looked over the mountains and could see so far away, there was no friends. It was a mystery to me how I could see that far and couldn't see the Indian reservation. I missed my dear friends. I knew in my heart that I would never get to see them again or get to go back to the reservation.

Papa and Uncle Clarence had cleared off a place big enough to put the cabin, and the oak, pine, and hickory trees were all in around us. They used giant oak logs for the walls and hued out notches where large, square nails were driven into the logs to hold them in place. Everything we had in our house was made out of wood—our beds, chairs, bed frames, and everything. Papa and Uncle Clarence had sawed our beds out of boards and made chairs out of big round pieces of wood—oak, I believe it was. Our table was a long table, about six foot long, and they made benches to go on both sides. It was real comfortable.

Our bed was clear across the back end of the cabin. It was built about four foot up off the dirt floor. Mama and Papa slept on one end of it, and us children slept on the other end. The Indians always kept their babies in with them for fear of animals and bad people comin' and gettin' them or stealing them in the night.

Mama made mattresses out of cotton-picking sacks she purchased for a nickel a piece. She sewed the sacks together and stuffed them with bear grass. There was a big field of open ground, and the bear grass would grow all over it. The pillows were made the same way. Both the mattresses and the pillows had to be swatted everyday with a switch to loosen them up and separate the grass so it would sleep comfortable.

We didn't have no storm cellar, but in Oklahoma, believe you me, we got some storms. To make it safe for us, Papa built in a place under the bed so if anything happened, or if anything went wrong like a storm come up, we would always be safe under there. Papa always looked out for the safety of the family.

Papa built us a stove out of two oil drums—for warming the cabin and cooking the food. Uncle Clarence built two chicken coops outside, up off of the ground to protect the chickens from the wolves, coyotes, and the coons. Otherwise, the wild animals would eat the eggs and the chickens. Papa also built a horse lot where the horses could stay in at night and eat and rest for the next day's work. He also built a watering trough from a black gum tree, where the horses could drink. Fresh water would come out of the mountains through two copper pipes—one to the black gum log trough where the horses would drink and the other at the house for us to use.

Papa got a job workin' for the Choctaw Lumber Company, haulin' big old logs and ties. He would take the train and, of course, it didn't cost him anything because he was workin' for the company. The train would come up the mountain every morning and go back in the evening about dinner time. It would blow so loud it'd almost bust your eardrum. It was a long and lonesome blow. *Oooh, Oooh*, it'd say. It seemed like the engineers'd especially blow the horn for us 'cause they knew we were there. We'd sit up on the stacks of railroad ties outside the cabin waiting for it to come and wave as it went by. We were always proud to hear it 'cause it meant our daddy was either going to work or coming home.

One particular mornin,' Mama made us all a nice big round hoecake apiece and set us down to the table. It was a beautiful sight. She sat on one of the sides of the table and Papa sat on the other. Here he is, he's tall and thin and got beautiful black hair and a red moustache—a very handsome feller. My mother is tall and thin and got real long black hair. She could stand up and her hair would lay about six inches on the floor, and she was six foot tall! You could just see the love rollin' all over their faces. They were sitting there smiling, holding hands. Papa said the blessing, and us children were all quiet as mice. He said, "Now you've always got to say your blessin's over your food. Even if no one is there to hear it but you, Jesus does. It will digest better and it will be better for you and you'll live longer."

I felt well-blessed and well-loved. To have a Papa and a Mama and everything beautiful. It was such a beautiful setting.

As we were eating there at the table, I asked Mama, "Why do they call them hoecakes?"

She replied, "Some people cook hoecakes over an open fire on the blade of a hoe to keep them from getting burned. That's where they got the name of the hoecake. 'Cause they were cooked on the hoe."

I thought about what Mama had said about the hoecakes and how right she was.

After we was done eatin' our food, Papa told Mama he had to go into town to get some supplies—grub and saw blades and things they needed. Papa got Uncle Clarence and they took off with the horses. They'd left pretty early that mornin', around ten o'clock.

It was such a beautiful time of the year. It was in the fall and the hickernuts had started to droppin' from the trees. Mama and us kids got out in the woods, and she let us take up our dress tails and pick up hickernuts. I remember it as well as if it was yesterday. We picked up the nuts, and then Mama took us back to the step where Papa had sawed off a flat log there for us to sit on, and we ate our hickernuts. Mama had taken one rock and put it on top of anothern', and we'd crack our nuts, and then she would show us how to take the meat out of the shells with a wooden pick. I loved the taste of hickernuts and felt real happy to gather them up with my mama. The pleasure was always with my mother.

Papa had a twelve-gauge shotgun, and he'd taught Mama how to use it. She could kill the animals for us to eat, or anything that would bother us. Papa said, "Now, man or beast, anything that comes here that you think will bother you and these children—you use that gun." He was real strict and strong about tellin' her.

This particular mornin' there was a squirrel up in the tree and so Mama killed the squirrel and dressed it out and cleaned it for meat. The way we had been raised was to live off the land. Well, it began to come in dark, and Mama had done cooked the squirrel and we'd all ate when we heard the biggest scream. It sounded like a woman screamin'. Everybody was scared. Mama grabbed us all, and we got back in under the bed in the storage place we had to keep our food and stuff from the animals. She looked real funny, but she put all of us children in under there for safety. We put our arms around each other and huddled together knowing that Mama would take care of us.

She got out Papa's shotgun, the old twelve-gauge that he had showed her how to use and, sure enough, about the second scream, that big old black panther stuck its head over the place where Papa hadn't quite finished all the roof on the house. We were peekin' where we could see what was goin' on. Mama backed up a little bit from where she was standin', and it left, or we thought it left. It was gone maybe twenty or thirty minutes and then we heard it again. It was on top of the house. This time it stuck its head and front parts down like it was gonna jump in there. Every one of us was trembling and shaking. Mama unloaded the shotgun on it. *BOOM! BOOM!*

That big old thing, you could hear it rollin' and slidin'. It sounded like a horse on top of the house. It fell down to the side of the house and of course Mama was scared to death. She reloaded the gun and got ready and she set right there with the gun ready to shoot anything that come through that door.

Papa heard the shots, and he turned that team loose and was runnin' as fast as he could come to see about us. When he got there, he called Mama, "Nannie, it's me, honey. What's the matter?"

She called back to him. "Fred, you watch out! I shot a big black cat off the house."

Then he hollered, "That must have been a panther!"

He looked and here was that big old huge thing—it must have weighed 140 or 150 pounds. It was as big as a sheep, or bigger.

Papa called out, "It's safe out here now," and Mama brought out the Coleman lantern to Papa to see what had happened.

He said, "You've got to be careful 'cause there's another'n. Where there's one, there's always two."

We went out and looked at it. She had shot that thing under its chin and blowed the whole top off of its head. I mean, really demolished it!

Papa gets the groceries and the hoes and the plows and things all out of the wagon, and he hooks up one of the mules and ties it on to it and hauls it away to the other side of the mountain.

Time went by, I guess two weeks, and we had to have some more supplies. My Uncle Clarence, bless his heart, he was a comin' home from gettin' us supplies and had got to a little crossin' in the creek, and he heard a racket in the tree. The next thing Clarence knowed, somethin' had jumped into the wagon and started for him in the springseat. He already had his single tree—the thing that hooks the horse up to the wagon—in his hands, ready for bear. He struck the panther with the single tree right between the eyes and killed it. This was all about a mile from the house, and when we heard the team a comin' all in a rush, Papa said something had surely happened.

Sure enough, when Uncle Clarence had got closer to the cabin he called out to Papa, "Fred, come out here! I think I've killed another cat!! He jumped out of the tree into the wagon, and I couldn't see and I struck him. I must have struck him a dozen times!"

Papa and Mama both went out to the wagon to see what he done. Well, that was another one of them black cats stretched out long, almost as long as the wagon. A great big thing. Papa said, "Well, there's the mate to the other'n.'"

Chapter Three
1924-1925

After we lived two years in the Kiamichi Mountains, Papa told Mama one mornin', "Nannie, we need to get these children out of the mountains back to civilization so they can get an education. They're gonna have to have an education to make it."

Well, Mama was like a little sheep and honored every word Papa said, and we began movin'. We were getting ready to leave the mountains and our little home, and I felt insecure and afraid of where we was to go and was wondering about it. I was going to miss the hollering of the wolves and the squirrels barking and the train whistling morning and night. I didn't want to leave. I wanted to stay there forever, but it was impossible because Papa wanted to get us an education.

We loaded up and got on the train, and we left the Kiamichi Mountains and went down to Alicia, Oklahoma. Papa and Mama had some friends that lived down there, and their name was McGowan. Mrs. McGowan was a very dear friend of my mother, and Mr. McGowan was a very dear friend to my father. We all loved each other and felt free to go there. Felt welcome. They had one small boy that was about twelve years old and two smaller girls. They were tickled to death to have us as company because back then you didn't have much company if you wasn't on the Indian reservation.

Mama was pregnant with our baby sister, and Papa was fixin' us a place to live. He was building a long shotgun house. It was about fourteen foot wide and about thirty-eight foot long. The first bedroom was on the back end of the house. The kitchen had a wood stove and a long table and our old chairs that we brought down from the mountains. You had to come through the front bedroom to get to the kitchen because there was no living rooms back then. We had an outside relief room because there was no such thing as bathrooms or toilets inside. Nobody had them.

As time went by, we moved into our new house, and Mama had the little baby girl, Ruth Irline. She was six weeks-old, and Mama found her dead in bed with her. She was so pretty. It was a terrible loss. My aunt and the doctor, too, said that mother's breast had fell over the baby's face and smothered her to death. The doctor searched her and couldn't find a bruise; he searched her all over. Of course, since then, after I got grown and had children of my own, I've had so much experience with life and people a losin' their babies with crib death, and I know that baby didn't die from Mama's breast fallin' over her face. That's almost impossible. Anyway, the loss of that baby was a grievin' Mama awfully bad.

One day, an Indian agent that signs you up for land and cows and chickens and things come to our house. He came to the door in Alicia. I got up and told Mama, "There's a man out here, and I think he's dead. He's got on black clothes."

Mama opened the door and said, "Oh, honey, this is the Indian agent. He's come to bring us some good news!"

Of course, I was just a little girl and wanted to know everything, and I sat in my little chair and paid real close attention to everything that was happenin' around.

He sit down and talked to Mama about being an Indian, and she said, "I'm a full-blood Choctaw Indian, Redbone."

He says, "Well, I will tell you now, Mrs. Morse, I'm going to write you up for some cows and chickens and later some hogs, but you'll have to get some pastures and things ready prepared before we can deliver them."

Whenevern' it came time for Mama to sign for her things, she didn't know how. Mama didn't read and write. That was the way it was. She made an X on the paper, and then the agent signed for her. Papa would always sign, but he was gone workin'. Papa was a well-educated man. He was an Indian agent, and that's how my mother and him met each other, my dad being an Indian agent. He'd been to all the colleges and a lot of things that people that don't read and write don't know about. He had a beautiful education.

They delivered the cows with a baby heifer calf, a good-sized bull calf, six white-legged chickens, and a rooster. The chickens laid the most beautiful white eggs. I'll never forget those eggs. Mama was real proud to get the chickens and the cows. Uncle Clarence built a cow pen and a henhouse, and Papa built a big rail fence about five foot tall, and that old bull jumped right over that fence and ran away.

That same day a man come by our house and told my daddy that some of our folks was down sick and maybe some of them dead with that swine flu. He needed help. I went with Papa, and it started raining—oh, it rained and it rained and stormed and lightning and thundered. We finally got over to some of the folks' houses which had already passed away. It was a sad thing.

During the meantime, Mama was out in all that rain, runnin' that bull. When we got back, Papa and my uncle got the bull back in pasture and put some barbwire around the top of it to keep the bull in the pen. But Mama, runnin' the bull in the rain, she took down with the swine flu. She was so sick coughin', and Papa was also sick, with pneumonia. I had appendicitis.

We all three had been sick in bed for three days when the doctor got out there. He ordered a block of ice on my back and legs from the waist down to keep my appendix from burstin' until they had time to get me to the nearest hospital. They never did take me to the hospital. It was about a hundred and thirty miles to Oklahoma City where the hospital was, and in a wagon or the train it would take too long to get me there.

I was frozen, and it was hurting like a sore thumb. My back and legs felt real numb. There was no good feeling in them at all. They finally took the ice off me and the swelling went down. Papa was in the kitchen in the bed, and I was in the living room in the bed—in my little kid bed. Mama was in the bed there in the room where I was at, about three foot from me. She wanted me close to her bed so she could talk to me. Sometimes she would hold my hand and talk to me about Jesus. She'd say, "I can always depend on Him."

She turned to me one day and told me, "Now, Nellie, you're the strong one of the bunch, and if something happens to me and Daddy you're gonna have to look after the rest of them. Keep everyone together. Don't get separated. You're gonna be strong. You have to do this. Hattie is little and sickly, and Edny is just a baby, and somebody's got to look after them. You're the only one I've got I can count on." Then she gave me a hug and started to cry. She put her head back down on her pillow, and in an hour's time she done gone. She done passed away.

My heart was falling out. It was awful. I was shakin' and cryin', and the tears were rolling down on my face to the end of my mouth. It was the most horrible experience that I'd ever had. With every breath I was praising God, and blessing God, and asking Him to help to see me through it so I could do what Mama had asked me to do—to take care of my two sisters. She left them both in my charge, and here I couldn't take a step if I had to.

I was already missing her rose perfume and all of her kindness and her calling, "Nellie, are you okay?" a dozen times a day, or more. She'd call me wanting to know if I was hungry or if I needed a drink of water or anything.

I thought of the warm blankets that she made me and wondered if there would ever be another one. I knew that I would miss my mother's love because I was sick, and she was always there with me. I knew that in her heart I was her special kid. She would always tell me that. She'd say, "Nellie, you're my special little girl." Though I couldn't walk, she made me feel wanted and special.

I felt I would miss my Mama more than my sisters because they could run and play, and I was right there through the whole situation with her. Before she passed away, I was with her every minute of the day, by her side. I was in my bed, and she was in her bed.

Mrs. McGowan and Mrs. Strickland—a friend that lived two doors down from where we lived—came and dressed Mama in a long, white dress, the one she was baptized in two weeks previous to her death. She looked just like an angel. They crossed her hands over her chest. Mrs. McGowan took Mama's right hand and laid it on her chest, and Mrs. Strickland then taken the left hand and laid it over the top of the right hand.

After we buried her over at Wright City Cemetery, we was all home—Papa and us three girls. Papa was still sick. He was so sick he couldn't say anything. It was so scary because I had lost my Mama, and it looked like I was going to lose my Papa, too. Some men in white clothes came and told him he would have to go with them. The doctor that ordered me to be in a block of ice had declared Papa with tuberculosis and said he would have to go to a TB sanitarium to be treated.

Chapter Notes

Alicia, Oklahoma:

Nellie and I visited her mother's grave in Wright City, Oklahoma, May 2007. The grave shows her mother's life span: 1899-1925. This information helped define the dates of this chapter and gave us an idea of how long her family had lived in the Kiamichi Mountains.

Chapter Four
1925

Our Aunt Leona, God rest her soul, took us kids home for about a week. That Sunday, she dressed us up real pretty and took us to the church. The minister got up and said, "We've got a problem in our neighborhood, and I'm gonna need some help. We've got three little girls, and their mother is dead and their father is in a TB sanitarium. Is there anybody that will take these three little girls?"

This man stood up and the woman did, too, and said, "We'll take 'em."

I think they was interested in earnin' a little extra money for havin' us in their home.

We stayed with this family for about a week. The woman bathed us, combed our hair, and told us how pretty we was. One day she asked us, "How was you children treated at home? Was they mean to you? Was they good to you?"

I was the talkative one of the bunch, and I said, "Oh, they loved us very much. Our Mama and our daddy loved us above all things in the world. And the Indians on the reservation loved each of us and they loved each other. They are good, kind people."

Then the woman asked me, "Nellie, how come your baby sister has big brown eyes and black hair, and your older sister has dark, curly hair and is dark complected?"

I said, "Our mother is full-blood Choctaw Indian. I heard her say so."

Suddenly the woman's whole outlook turned around. She taken disposition against it, and when her husband come in that evening, she said, "Do you know what we've done? We've taken into our home some damn little Indian children. These kids aren't white kids, they're damn little Indians."

I knowed I'd said the wrong thing then.

Well, the husband began to beat on her for it. He began to hit her and beat her, and he finally beat her until he got her in a corner, and he just stood there and kicked her. Kicked her in the face and in the arms and legs. They had a twelve-year-old boy, and he run off to get help. The woman finally got in the closet and got away from him, I guess it was a grocery closet, or something. Anyway, she got the door shut, and he couldn't kick her no more. Me and my sisters gathered in a little corner and were scared to death, afraid he was going to turn on us girls. We didn't know nothin' about people fighting like that. We'd never seen nothing like it before.

Well, it come night, and some men in white clothes, the Ku Klux men come and got him and took that man out there in just seeing distance and tied him to a pine tree, and they whooped him with a horsewhip. They whipped him and beat him and told him, "You're gonna work and make your wife a fat-old livin'. You're not a gonna hit your wife no more."

And they would hit him and hit him, and they beat him until whenevern' they cut him lose, he fell to the ground. He crawled, he did not walk back to the cabin where we was at, he crawled. The wife washed him and cleaned him up a little bit.

Early the next mornin', a man and woman that run the orphanage come to the house. The orphanage man says, "I've come after the girls."

She was a kind woman, and she taken our blankets and quilts and put them in the back end of the wagon. We had about a change of clothes. That's about what we had when we got there to the house. The man from the orphanage said, "You kids are gonna have to get down."

He couldn't stand for one of us to say something or make any noise. If we were talkin' or cryin', he'd say, "I'll tape your mouth shut, I'll tape your mouth shut."

Or he'd say, "I'll throw you into the hog pen to the hogs if you don't stop it."

Two weeks went by, and we went back to church, and my Aunt Leona was there. She'd just sit there and never even cracked a smile or a grin whenevern' they'd given us away like little dogs. She had three girls of her own, and she was pregnant, so she said she didn't have room for us and she couldn't afford us. She kept lookin' at me. I wanted to tell her that I wasn't mad at her for givin' us away like little dogs. I loved her. That's all I wanted to say, and I broke down and cried.

After the service was over, we started home, back to the orphanage. It seemed to me like about three miles from the church. I don't know really 'cause I was too little to know that. After the church service, we all got in the wagon. Our dresses were made of flour sacks, and our underwear was made of rough cracker sacks that rubbed my legs raw. My skin was sensitive anyway. I didn't have any shoes.

The old man who took us was wearin' a blue coat with silver stripes, plain dark blue pants, and a black hat with a flat rim. He was very scary looking. He had dark brown hair and ice-cold, blue-gray eyes that were set close together. They almost looked cross-eyed. He had a square jaw and a long, thin pointy nose. Most of his teeth were rotten and chipped, and the pieces that were left were stained a dark yellah color from smokin'. He had dirt under his fingernails and caca breath from smokin' cigars and cigarettes. He took brown paper and rolled tobacco inside the paper and would smoke it. It left the most horrible stench on his clothes and breath. He was so mean, he wasn't human, he was an animal. His little old wife was barely five feet tall, and he treated her horribly mean. He bossed her around and swore at her all the time.

There were two springseats in the wagon. One for the old man, and the other seat was for the man's wife and the little old colored lady that worked at the orphanage. The old man throwed my chair up to the back end of the wagon, and my sisters set in the back end on some pillows and quilts and things.

When we got close to the house, instead of going to the house, he turns up next to the hog pen, and he looked at me and said to his wife, "Get out! I'm gonna teach this one a lesson!"

As soon as they got out of sight, he jerked my panties off of me and raped me right there on that springseat and told me if I told anybody he'd kill me. But when he jerked my panties off, he throwed them in the hog pen, and the hogs was grabbin' them. The fear of what was happenin' brought forth my mother's voice, and she began to hum in a soft, tender voice, "When the roll is called up yonder, I'll be there."

Let us labor for the Master from the dawn till setting sun,
Let us talk of all His wondrous love and care;
Then when all of life is over, and our work on earth is done,
And the roll is called up yonder, I'll be there.

I know my mother was gone, but she was yet with me.

Whenevern' he got through rapin' me, he threw me over in that hog pen where there were about three or four wild hogs. I began to scream, and the angels lifted me up and took me away from the hogs and put me up on the fence. At that time, those wild hogs was still jumpin' up, tryin' to get to me. This little colored lady, she heard me screamin' and cryin', and she come and got me. I was bloody from the top of my head to the bottom of my feet, and my clothes was tore all off of me.

She took me and bathed me and cleaned me up. I was still whimperin' and cryin', and the old man told me, "I'll kill both of your sisters if you say one word—one word!"

And every time after that when he would rape me, he would say, "I'll either give your sisters away, and I'll take care of you here myself, or I will kill both of them. Your daddy ain't never comin' back. You might as well get that in your head right now."

I have markings on my feet and legs today and a place on top of my head that still got scars on it. I could show somebody if they wanted to see it, still yet, and I'm eighty-eight years old. The signs and abuse that he put on me is still there right now.

Life at the orphanage was hard. The man's wife was in charge of keeping me busy with different tasks to do around the farm. Because of my polio, I couldn't get up and get around like the other kids, but they would set down one hundred pound sacks of Irish potatoes or a big basket of old onions that would get in my eyes. I had to sit there and peel those onions and things because we had about twelve colored people—men and women—workin' on the farm that needed feedin'.

Sometimes I would help the colored lady with washing. She was in charge of doing the laundry for the twelve workers in the fields. My arms would get tired because the big wet overalls that belonged to them were heavy, and I would have to hang them up on the clothes line.

The old man treated her like a dog, just like the rest of us. Sometimes the colored lady took my two sisters to town with her to run errands, and the old man would say to her, "You leave Nellie behind; I'll take care of her here."

I knew what those words meant.

My sisters and I slept in bunk beds out in the service porch. We slept on toe sacks that were stuffed with hay and used blankets that belonged to my mother. The shed we slept in was enclosed, but it still got real cold.

I would always have a prayer with my sisters before we got into bed each and every night. We always said our prayers and call our mama and our papa's name and ask God to look over them and watch over us three little girls.

The workers slept in a separate bunk house on the property. We weren't allowed to talk to them. If they weren't working hard enough, the old man would make them get on the ground, and he would whip them with a horsewhip. Sometimes he'd put the ones that didn't work hard enough on a diet of bread and water to try and teach them a lesson. I worried about them being hungry and abused, and my heart and soul went out to the whole situation. I asked for blessings for the colored people, and at the same time I asked for blessings for me and my sisters.

But, this little colored lady, every once in a while, she'd come by me and whisper, "You've got to have faith, you've got to hold on for your sisters' sake. You've got to hold on. One of these days, you're gonna look up and your daddy is gonna be comin' up that road right there. You remember what I'm tellin' you. Jesus is not a gonna let us down. The spirits is gonna be with us for always. Not just today and tomorrow, but for always."

These were the kindest words I heard in the three months I was at the farm

Sometimes people came by to look at us. The old man's wife would dress my sisters up and braid their hair and try to sell my sisters or give them away. I had to stay in a corner at the backside of the house where I was out of sight because they were ashamed of me. The old man would say, "No one wants a crippled kid."

I felt defeated. I felt alone and afraid.

There were plenty of other times me and my sisters had to stay in back out of sight—during the holidays, and if people came by to visit the old man and his wife. They didn't want us out bothering them so they would put us in the back room and come whip us if they heard us talking.

Sure enough, the old man and woman taken a notion that spring to go away and lock us up in the storm cellar. They were only gonna be gone for that one day. Well, there was a big flash flood, or something, and they didn't get back for four days. On the third day, that little old colored lady, God rest her soul, and one of the boys broke the lock on the storm cellar and got us out. They had to carry my baby sister out in their arms. She was so weak she couldn't even stand up. Of course, with my legs being what they were, they carried me out, too.

The days to come, while I was sitting there workin,' peelin' onions to be exact, and I looked up that road and there was my daddy! He was comin' after us! I thought I was seeing a spirit. When he got to us, he grabbed me and hugged and kissed me. It was the first good hug I'd had since he and Mama had been gone. It had been almost three months. I don't like to cry, but it was a blessing to see our papa coming. He grabbed my sisters, and he said, "You won't stay another night here! You'll never stay another night with nobody besides me. I've come to take you home."

I was so thankful and happy and knowed the Lord had sent our papa back to us.

Chapter Notes:

Words of Nellie: "Mrs. McGowan and Mrs. Strickland would have been at church, and they would have been the ones who took us, but they both stayed home on account of illness in the family. They caught the swine flu. Everybody had the swine flu. They asked everyone that had someone sick in the family with the swine flu to stay home because people were just dying all over the place. Mrs. Strickland come almost to losin' Mr. Strickland during the swine flu. It was a killer.

"Aunt Leona Mae Bailey had three girls of her own, and was about six months pregnant with a baby boy. She lost him through the flu. She couldn't take us because she said six kids would have been too much responsibility."

Chapter Five

1926

My daddy came and got us from the orphanage, and he carried us back to the McGowan's. They are good, fine, lovin' people. Of course, they were Indians, too, and one Indian will love another'n' and understand what's going on. We moved next door to a lady by the name of Mrs. Walker. Mrs. Walker had taken our cows and chickens and everything after Mother died and the men took Papa away to the sanitarium.

Mrs. Walker told Papa that she would take care of us children early in the morning while he worked. He was to give her a dollar a week to take care of all three of us. My oldest sister, Hattie, got old enough to where she was going to school, and I would have been going to school, too, but I had the old Polio that kept me from walking. I was mostly stranded.

Mrs. Walker didn't come to see us one particular morning, and so Hattie and my baby sister, Edna, said, "We're hungry, Nellie."

I said, "Well, I remember what Mama had done. I remember Mama making the biscuits."

Hattie said, "Do you think you can make the biscuits?"

"If you go and get the stuff, then I can make the biscuits," I said.

She got me Mama's bread pan, and she put the flour in. I taken my little hand and I raked that around, and then I put in a pinch of salt and a pinch of Clabber Girl baking powder. Hattie read it off, "Clabber Girl." We added milk from the cow and mixed this in.

I went ahead and made up the biscuits and rolled 'em in the cooking oil and put them in the pan. When it come time to get the dough off my hands, I couldn't get it off. I didn't watch Mama do that part of it, and Hattie and Edny weren't interested in what Mama was doing, so they didn't no how to get it off either. It was really funny. I began to swing my hands, and I got dough all over the house. I still didn't get it all off. Finally Mrs. Walker come and she said, "What on earth are you doing?"

I said, "I can't get this dough off my hands."

"Come right over here, and we'll get this wash basin and a wash pan," she told me.

I wet my hands real good and it begin to comin' off. She got over close to me, and I began to wipe my hands on her apron. Strange enough, everybody called her "Greasy Walker." The reason they did is because she wore an old apron, and every time her hands got dirty she would wipe 'em on this apron. I thought, *Oh, my goodness! I'd soon to have the dough on my hands as this dirty rag!* Mama was pretty clean with everything and pretty particular with us children.

My two sisters pulled my chair over in front of the oven door to where I could see if the biscuits was brown. Our stove was a little homemade stove Papa had made out of a fifty-gallon barrel and a five-gallon bucket. I told them, "When the biscuits turn brown, then they're done."

When they got brown we took them out. I told my sisters, "Now you take the spoon and open the biscuits, and then you take a little bit of the butter and put it in there and put us some jelly in there, too." We ate every last one of those biscuits.

When Papa come home, he said, "My goodness, what in the world have you kids been into?"

Hattie said, "Nellie made us some biscuits, Papa. You can whoop Nellie. She done it."

Papa was kinda chuckling, and he says, "We're gonna let Nellie slide this time."

* * * * *

Mrs. Walker's sister, Lula Chauncey, would come up from Arkansas to visit her often, and she became acquainted with Papa. Papa and her got to seein' each other every time she'd come see Mrs. Walker. They finally decided to get married.

Our family moved to Richmond, Arkansas, into a big house where Lula (we called her Mrs. Morse) lived. Mrs. Morse stayed on Mr. Perry's farm and helped him tend to his animals and crops in exchange for living accommodations. Mr. Perry liked Papa and hired him to keep the farm up. He gave us chickens, a cow, and a hog, and he also asked Papa, "How would you like to share crop my land? I'm too old to work it now, and I'd be happy to have you."

He seen that Papa was a good worker. Papa was very intelligent and had worked and made lots of good money, but he put it all behind him to raise us three girls—he put the whole world behind him, it looked like. He laid his life down for ours.

This woman Papa married was real strict and hateful and mean, and she was real hard on us. Well, we had a Mama and our Mama died, and Mrs. Morse wasn't nothin' like our Mama. We didn't want to call her mama. She told us, "If you can't call me mama, then you're gonna have to call me Mrs. Morse."

She had long, stringy hair that was kind of a dark brown, and deep, grey eyes. She always acted and talked like she was mad at the world and treated us girls awfully bad. She had a long, gathered skirt, and her bloomers come down below her knees, like a short-legged pair of britches. Whenever' she would run, she'd catch her skirt and pull it up, and her bloomers would show, and she thought that looked sexy. I think it looked disgusting. She couldn't speak a kind word to us children.

During the time Papa and Mrs. Morse lived together we were not allowed to speak the Choctaw language. If she caught us speaking Choctaw she would heat a fork on the stove and touch it to our tongue until it made smoke rise off our tongue. I still yet have a place on my bottom lip where the hot fork stuck to my lip and took all the meat off. She had to jerk on it to get it loose, and my lip was sore for months and months. When Papa asked me what was the matter with my lip, Mrs. Morse spoke up and said, "Oh, Nellie chews on her lip all the time."

And Hattie spoke up and said, "Papa, that's a lie. She burnt Nellie's mouth with a fork."

Then I went and showed Papa the fork that she stuck on my lip, and that was the end of their good marriage. It lasted between three and four months long. Papa raised us girls the rest of the way by hisself.

Mrs. Morse moved away and Papa continued workin' Mr. Perry's farm, plowin' the fields, raisin' the cotton, raisin' the corn and peanuts, and everything. Papa also had a little place there on the end of the porch where he fixed the guns and the pots and the pans and the sewing machines. I was right there by his side helping him. He always found a place for me. Of course he worked in guns until he knowed every part about a gun. He taught me how to take a gun apart and how to put it together, how to make the guns' stocks out of curly walnut, and how to cut 'em out.

I could do all kinds of little jobs, though I couldn't walk a step. I could wash dishes if they got me close enough to the pan, or if they'd pull me around, I could make the bed. There was many things that I could do to help, but there were many things I couldn't do, and I acknowledged that.

Whenevern' I would be there with Papa, why I would watch the ducks come and go to the creek. They followed one right after another. Usually a drake would take the lead, and the rest would all follow. They would lay their eggs along the way from the house to the creek. There were green eggs and there were white eggs. The drakes would have a green head and a green neck and the hens was a beautiful brown color.

Chapter Notes

Bond for Marriage License: Fred J. Morse to Lula Chauncey, County of Little River, May 10, 1926, Ashdown, Arkansas. Finding this certificate helped us place the time when Nellie and her family moved from Oklahoma to Ashdown and also helped us calculate how long Nellie and her sisters were at the orphanage.

Chapter Six
1927

After everything was said and done, I was still bound to the chair. I had been down so sick for so long and was thin and poor. One morning, I woke up with a really bad fever and chills, and Papa was worried about me, so he went to a little place called Richmond and got a doctor by the name of Doctor Ringo. Well, Doctor Ringo was an alright doctor, I guess. He taken one look at my swollen stomach, and he give Papa some yeast tablets for me to take so I could burp. That's what it amounted to, so I could burp up the air. I don't know if he thought I couldn't hear him, but he went out into the hallway, and I heard him tell Papa, "There ain't one more thing you can do, Mr. Morse, you've done all you can. You can't save her. You might as well get a burial ground and get ready for it."

He must have stayed there an hour, declaring me being dead. He told Papa, "Whenevern' she passes on, I'll be here to declare it."

Papa said, "Yes, sir; yes, sir."

I thought to myself, *You just don't know what you're talking about. I know that the Lord can help me, and I'm gonna ask Him to.*

Papa got ready and headed old Doctor Ringo back to Richmond—between three and five miles—it was a good ways up there and back. Papa had been gone about thirty minutes, and I cried out to God and said, "Oh,

Lord, please help me get better." Just when I finished my prayer, I heard somebody step up on the porch and I heard a light knock on the door. I heard whoever it was turn around, and it sounded like they were leavin.' I cried out, Oh, Lord Jesus, please don't leave me now, I need your help. Please don't leave me; I can't get out of this chair. Please, come in!" Sure enough, he opened the door and peeked his head 'round the corner. He said, "Young lady, you're stuck in that chair."

I said, "I'm sick, and I've been here a long time."

He was a warm man. He was about five feet, eight inches tall and broad shouldered. He was Cherokee Indian. He had a long black braid as thick as my fist run down his back all the way to his waist. His beard was black and grey, and his eyes were a deep dark brown. His smile was warm. He was wearin' a tan buffalo hide skin jacket and britches to match. The jacket had fringe runnin' across the front and underneath the arms. And he was wearin' moccasins that laced halfway up his leg and were tied with hide strings

He come in, and, oh, he smelt bad. He smelt like he hadn't had a bath in a long time. He said "Little lady, I've got to have somethin' to eat. I haven't had a bite to eat in three days and nights."

I said, "Well, you've come to the right place. Papa said there was a pot of black-eyed peas and hound-hogs on the stove and a big pan of cornbread in there on the oven door stayin' warm. There are onions hangin' on the wall. Just take a knife and cut you off one of them big old white Pamutti onions to eat with it. In the well is where we keep our milk to keep it cold. You get you a bucket to get you some milk. There's good milk out there—good, cold buttermilk."

He kinda got a little grin on his face, and he said, "Yes, Ma'am!"

He turns and goes and gets his milk and a plate, then leans up against the wall and ate. He ate like he was starvin' to death. It almost looked like he swallowed the food whole. He ate and ate until he was full. I believed he was hungry! Then he come and stood right in front of me and said, "Little lady, you've got polio. How would you like to walk again?"

"That's what the doctor said," I told him. "But the doctor also said I'm dyin'. Why would I want to walk if I'm dyin'?"

"Well, I asked you a question, don't ask me one," he said. "How would you like to walk?"

"Oh, it would be the greatest thing on earth if I could just walk!"

"I've come to your assistance," he said. "You fed me, I'll cure you."

He seemed to know just exactly what he was a talkin' about.

He set against the wall and pushed a little wooden stool Papa had made for people to sit on, up against the wall and kinda dozed off to sleep. He was a big old Indian chief, he was just as pretty as he could be, but he sure did smell bad. I heard Papa come in with the team, and I called the man, "Mister, you can wake up now!" Papa put the mare up, her name was Nell, and he come in.

I told Papa, "This man was hungry, and you told me never turn nobody away that was hungry."

"Good girl," Papa said. "If you turn somebody away and they're hungry, you might turn Jesus away just as well. That's the truth."

By that time the man was hearin' Papa's voice and woke up. He raised up off the stool and said, "And your name is Mr. Morse?"

"Yes," Papa said.

"Mr. Morse, how would you like for your daughter to be well and be able to run and play?"

I'm a thinkin', *Oh, Papa, please don't say no!*

"Oh, God, yes! Oh, yes!" Papa said.

"Well, I better be on my way then and I'll go back to the Indian reservation," the man said. "I'll be back here at the settin' of the sun on the third day."

I knowed that man knowed what he was talkin' about.

Sure enough, the sun was about an hour from goin' down and here come this man with an old bear skin draped across his shoulders and a sack of weeds in his arms. He told Papa, "Let's wash out this washpot." They taken some lye soap that Papa had made and washed out the pot good and clean, but he never shook the dirt off them roots. I thought, *My goodness—as nasty as them weeds are, why are they washin' out the pot to get it clean?* Then they drawed clean water out of the well. They must have put about ten gallon in that washpot and boiled it. He taken the herbs out of the croaker sacks and pushed them down in the boilin' water, and he boiled them all night long. Papa had an old rockin' chair, and they cut a hole out so I didn't have to move if my kidneys or my bowels acted up.

Next thing, the medicine man wrapped me in some old cotton pickin' sacks. Papa had taken some cotton pickin' sacks, bleached them out, and sewed them together to make a blanket. He wrapped me in this. Then he wrapped me in the bear skin so no air could get in or out. He set me out like this on a chair in the hot Arkansas sun in July for three days. If you've ever been to Arkansas in July, you know how miserably hot it can be.

I woke up the next mornin' and my mouth was like cotton. I was so dry. He got two cups made out of tin cans, and he poured that weed water backwards and forth, and backwards and forth 'til it was cool enough where he thought I could drink it. He gave me about two tablespoon full. I drank it. I said, "Oh…that is so bitter!"

He said, "But it's gonna cure you. You've got to have faith. It's gonna cure you."

On the second day, my bowels moved, and he asked my sister to come and clean me up. I was miserably hot and could barely move. He continued to give me the boiled weed liquid throughout the day, and he never left my side for three days. He kept a fire underneath the pot to keep the liquid warm. That Indian man stayed right with me. He stayed in there and never backed off one bit. He doctored me, and he kept declaring, "This is going to cure you, you've got to have faith. You've got to have all the faith in the world, sister. I know you understand that I'm a healer through God, through the great spirits, and I'm a spiritual man. You fed me, and I'm gonna see you well."

On the third day, the old Indian medicine man stripped the bearskin off me, and underneath I was soaking wet. The blanket that used to be white was now a golden yellah color from the poisons that my body had gotten rid of. My sister Hattie said, "Oh, my goodness, you've ruined our one and only sheet!"

He said, "No, a little soap and water will take it right out."

He stood right in front of me and told me he was gonna stand me up. He caught me in under my arms, pulled me up out of that chair, and stood me on my feet. He said, "I'm gonna take three steps backward, and you need to take three steps forward, and I don't want you to stop walkin'." He had on old Indian moccasins, and I was watchin' his feet to make sure I didn't miss nothin'. I was so weak because I'd had nothing to eat for three days. I began to pray and ask Jesus for His help.

He stepped back three steps, and I stepped the three steps forward and fell in his arms. My sisters all shouted and hollered, "Yeah! You can walk! You can walk!" I was so happy to think I could walk.

I started in from that day on. Oh, it was miserable—my legs and arms and feet just felt like they was gonna come apart. But it wasn't long until I could walk clear across the house, and then I could walk out in the yard and around. It was just beautiful to be able to walk.

He said, "I want you to continue for the rest of your entire life—walkin', praisin' God, thankin' Him for doin' this. You know you owe Him a lot."

"Yes," I said, "I know I do."

I promised God at that time that if there ever was anybody that needed help, I intended to bless others just as well and I intended to take God all the way through with me, and I've done just that.

That man had sweated the polio poisons out of my system. He healed my body of the polio, and put me in God's hands to see that I walked and to see that I did the things that needed to be done in my life. Whenevern' he asked me if I had faith in God, my answer was always yes. He told me, "If you've got faith in God, after this treatment I'm gonna stand you on your own two feet and you will walk."

Chapter Notes:

Cushman, *History of the Choctaw, Chickasaw, and Natchez Indians*, p. 172. "When the traditional Indian doctor, called *alikchi* in Choctaw, was called to treat a patient, he did not take his medicines with him. He would first see the patient, make a diagnosis, and then decide if he could help. If he decided in the affirmative, he went immediately to the woods to gather the proper roots or herbs for the patient. After the medicine man prepared the medicines, he stayed with the patient until he either recovered or died."

Chapter Seven

1927

At church, Papa had a friend and his name was Mr. Sanders. He told Papa one day, "We've got four children, and my wife Cordelia is havin' a fifth one, and we really need some help. I can't work and make a livin' and take care of her and those kids, too."

I heard the frustration in his voice toward that woman and those poor little children, and she was having the fifth one. I thought to myself, *Now, God helped me. He put me back on my feet, and he's taught me how to walk. I could put one foot in front of the other'n' and walk. I was so blessed.* When Mr. Sanders left, I told Papa that I would like to go up there to these peoples' house and help them.

My daddy, he hooked up the team to the wagon, and he took me up to Cordelia's place, a little farm house about four miles west of Mr. Perry's house. I saw all those children, they were beautiful children, but I never saw a big family so nasty in my life. One of the little boys looked like he had scales on his legs, he was so dirty. That was the oldest one.

The house smelled musty and nasty. It had a terrible smell, and this woman was bigger than a barrel, and there was nothin' she could do about it, and the children didn't have the knowledge to help. So, I started in. I taken' a little hatchet and cut down some brush straw and made a broom and trimmed it to where I could sweep out the house. I wore blisters on my hands tryin' to get the dirt out of that house. But the kids, I'd tell them, "You pick this up and put it in that old barrel. You pick that up," and they would do it.

I started washin' dishes to cook. They had a double sink, and both sinks were stacked high with dirty dishes. Of course, there wasn't no soap. I couldn't find nothin' in the house. I wasn't too knowledged of a lot of things like other children would have been, to scrub pots and pans and plates. I taken all the dishes outside the house and got a big old washtub and put all the dishes in there. We'd take the dishes out one at a time and wash the plates real good with the sand and a rag and put them over in another tub to rinse them. It took all day long for me and the kids to wash the dishes to get them to where we could eat off of them.

That worked. It cleaned them and I thank God because there wasn't no way we could use those dishes. I don't know how Cordelia made it that long. It didn't look like that man ever turned his hand to do anything. It seemed like he come home long enough to get her pregnant and then he'd go off and leave her and the little kids to the mercy of the world.

When I woke up the next mornin', I was layin' on the floor in the corner of the kitchen on a quilt that the little boy had brought me. Cordelia was coughin' and struggling, trying to get her breath. I brought her a drink of water. She broke down to cry and said, "My husband has just left me and said he doesn't want nothing to do with another baby." Then she went on and told me she just wanted to die.

I felt sorry for her to think that she was left in a condition like this. My heart poured out to her. I wanted to comfort her. I took her hand in mine, and I begin to pray and told her to pray too. But, she was crying so hard and deep she wasn't getting many words out to God. I went ahead and prayed for her. Then I told her, "Cordelia, you're gonna make it through this. You don't want to die. You'd leave these children in the same mess you're in." I give her a little cloth.

"Wipe away your tears and straighten up your face. With God's help, I will see you through this."

There was a feeling in the room like all tears was gone and the Lord had begin to straighten things out and take over.

There was an assurance that we would make it.

So I started in. I said to myself that this family has got to have clean clothes—we've got to have soap, but there wasn't no money to buy soap with. A man would work all day for a dollar. I mean, all day for a dollar. From sun up to sun down for one dollar, and a lot of times he would have to take his pay in pumpkins, chickens, honey, or syrup, or something else. I knowed because my daddy would do that.

So, I talked to Papa. He come to see about me. He said, "How you doin', Square?" Of course, when I was little, why he give me my nickname, and I carried it as long as he lived. Most all Indians have a nickname, and mine was Square because no matter what happened, I would always tell the truth about it.

I told Papa, "I need some soap. I can't get these clothes clean without it."

He said, "Well, we'll go down back to the fields where I've been a cuttin' some old oak trees down and we'll get some ashes and make some lye. Of course, it's gonna take a day or two, but you do the best you can 'til we can get it made."

So he started in. We went down there and got about a five-gallon can of oak ashes and started drippin' the lye. We taken a screen and put it over our washtub. Papa put me a drip up over it to drip the water through a bucket with some holes in it, just so it would drip all day and all night. As that dripped out into the washtub it was an old, red, slick lye.

We built a great big fire around a washpot and gathered up all the grease substance that we could find, and measured it as we put it into the pot. We put about four cups of grease to one cup of lye, then draw the fire back to where it would set there and cook and bubble all day and all night. Whenevern' it would get to where it was real heavy—bubbles comin' from the bottom—we had to keep this stirred. Somebody had to stay with it and stir it constantly to keep it from sticking to the bottom of the washpot. My daddy had made a paddle out of good, dry pine, and we would take the paddle and stick it in there and push down to the bottom and bring it all up. Several times during the cooking, whenevern' it would go to bubblin', we'd put the baking soda in it. That made it foam and float and made it pretty and white.

We taken the big paddle used for stirrin' and let the soap drip into a pan of water to see how near done it was. If it dissolved it wasn't done. If it went into a little round ball and floated to the top you would consider it done. We would stir it until it was real thick. We had the fire real low so it wouldn't burn or catch on fire.

Then, old smart me, that old lye soap just smelled awful to have to put on your face and hands, so I went out and gathered a lot of rose blooms and some magnolia blooms and put them in a pan and put water on them—rain water at that. I did a pan each of lilacs, roses, and magnolias. I let them sit all night, and then I'd drain the water off. I'd take off the very top of the soap where it was pretty and white, then add some of the perfumes from the flowers and beat it up real good. I hadn't been out in the world very much, but I knowed if it smelled good, it would be better. I put the soap in a wooden box Papa had made.

It smelt so good and so pretty. And, it was as white as snow. The baking soda cleaned it and made it white. It was the first perfume soap I'd ever seen or knew about.

I cut some of the soap in bars to clean the house or things with, and then I cut little blocks to put in the wash pot full of hot water to wash the clothes in. That there lye soap would take the dirt and the filth right out of them.

Of course, we used a tub and rub board to clean the clothes 'cause in those days there weren't no such thing as a washing machine or a dryer. Everything had to be put in a washpot and boiled clean. That's the way we cleaned things.

Whenevern' I'd get ready to scrub the floor, I would take one of the little bars of soap and put it in a pan of hot water and those old pine floors would come so pretty and white. They'd come so clean.

After I got all the clothes washed, I taken a number three washpot and set it outside and the sun would warm the water. I taken and washed each one of those four kids. I started in with the oldest boy, Henry, and honest to goodness, he hadn't had a bath in so long until the dirt looked like scales on his legs. I made him sit in the wash tub a good while and kept the girls all in the house while he soaked. I got him all washed and got his clothes all boilin' and everything and got him all wrapped up in a towel so he could go in the house and look after the baby until his clothes dried.

I began washing one kid at a time, and washin' their clothes until I got all those kids washed in that one tub of water. It was just like chocolate soup! I didn't know. I had been handicapped from the polio and everything so long that I didn't know I had to change water for every kid. I couldn't have done it anyway. I couldn't have drawed that much water out of the well. It would've killed me!

Some of the fine city ladies from in town came out there one day and according to them, "this had to be done," and "that had to be done." I said, "I'm not being smart at you, but how about some of ya'll helping a little bit? It would really be appreciated. And bring some clothes if you've got anything you can't use or can't wear."

One of the women turned up her nose and said, "I don't have to take this!"

I said, "No, Ma'am, I didn't ask you to take this. I asked you to help me. This woman and kids need help. They've been needin' help for a long time, and it wouldn't hurt some of yu'ns to come out and see about them."

We was fifteen miles out of town right out in the country. We didn't get no help, but I went ahead and stayed there and done the best I could until she had that baby. Of course, being so handicapped for so long, it wore me plum out. I was still awfully weak from being sick. I sat and did a lot of things. I sewed and mended the kids' clothes and helped the lady. She'd cry—I felt so sorry for her.

Finally, months went by, and Cordelia had the little baby girl. I never will forget her name. They named her Elizabeth. I thought that was a pretty name, and it was my grandmother's name. She said, "Since you've been so good to me, if you think that's pretty Nellie, I am gonna name that baby Elizabeth." I thought that was the sweetest thing I ever heard—somebody would do something that I wanted done for a change.

During that week, the last week of November, the woman's brother-in-law come in, and he was a lot of help—getting the wood in for the winter, helpin' and doin'.

I don't think Mr. Sanders ever came back. If he ever did come back to the country I never heard about it. We give them meat, corn, peanuts—as much as we had to spare from my daddy's farmin'. Everything we had to spare, why we would try to turn it to help them. She was awful grateful. She really loved me and appreciated my help.

I felt like I had been sent to her on a mission as an angel. It was very hard and very tiring on me, and there were days that I would get so tired I couldn't walk a step, but I would call on God to help me, and that's the way we made it through the summer. Without the strength of God, I could have never made it. But I promised God that if He'd help me, I would help others.

Chapter Notes:

Here is a census of the family Nellie helped out.

Fifteenth Census of the United States: April 23, 1930. Little River County, Arkansas

Sanders, William   (Head)

Sanders, Cordelia   (Wife)

Sanders, Henry G.   (Son)

Sanders, Fannie   (Daughter)

Sanders, Lucinda   (Daughter)

Sanders, Albert   (Son)

Sanders, Elizabeth (Daughter)

Chapter Eight
1928

I helped Papa gather the corn and peanuts, and we put them in the barn so we would have them for the winter. Everybody had to prepare back then. They canned everything they could and saved everything they could to keep from starvin' to death through the winter. Papa always said, "Don't be like the grasshopper and eat all your food in the summer and have none for the winter."

After we got the crops all in, Papa come up to our bedroom one mornin' and sit down on the side of the bed. I looked up, and he had a great big smile on his face, and he was lookin' down at me. He said, "How would you girls like to start school?"

We shouted and cried at the same time and said, "Yes! Yes! Yes! We would love it, Papa!"

We all wanted to go to school.

He built a sled out of an oak tree and put in a seatbelt so I couldn't fall out because I couldn't stand up too good. He would get up every mornin' and hitch Nell, our old mare we had, to the sled and us three girls would pile on—me, Edny, and Hattie. It was about two-and-a-half miles to the school from where we lived. There was a creek below our house, and we would cross the creek over the bridge and then head on out up the hill to the schoolhouse.

The roads were winding—they were all wagon roads. They were all beat out and bumpy. There wasn't no such thing as concrete or blacktop back then. It was like ridin' a bucking horse on the sled because the roads were so bad. There was four houses between our house and the schoolhouse. The second house we come to was my new school teacher's house. She always rode the buggy to school.

The schoolhouse was a long, shot-gun building with red brick and stairs up to the front door. All the children in the schoolhouse met in one big classroom. Papa took us into the room to meet the teacher for the first time. We trailed behind him like little ducks. I was wearing blue and white striped overalls and moccasins on my feet. I had a brown coat with a fur collar. Papa held me by the hand, then Hattie, then Edny, and led us into the classroom and turned us over to Mrs. McGraw to teach us.

Mrs. McGraw told Papa, "Mr. Morse, I'll take good care of your daughters, and I appreciate them coming to school."

Mrs. McGraw took me and Hattie both to the fourth grade row and sat us both down, and she put Edny two rows over, in the primer row. There was five rows of desks, and each row of children would have different books and be learning a little different education.

"Good morning, children. I am Mrs. McGraw. I am your school teacher," she said that first day. Then everybody that wanted to repeat her words stood up and said, "Good morning, Mrs. McGraw."

Then she said, "You are all going to listen to what I have to say, and we're all going to get along, and we're all going to get our lessons."

I didn't have no book, but Mrs. McGraw would loan me one. She was a tall, thin woman and wore a long, black skirt and a white blouse with a round collar. She was just like an angel. Her hair was light brown, and she had it pulled back away from her face and crossed over in the back. She had beautiful dimples wedged in the sides of her mouth. I thought she was suckin' in on her jaws to make the dimples, so I tried it. I tried to make me some dimples, and I sucked so hard on my jaws I made a blister inside my mouth.

I looked around to take notice. My daddy had always told me to be aware of the things around me. My little chair was made out of cane and sweet gum posts, and the bottoms of the other chairs was just a plain board. Mine was different because the other wood would have probably deformed my hips. That's what Papa said.

There was a big, black slate board on the wall behind Mrs. McGraw, and down in the tray there was a lot of chalk pieces. The sweetest thing I ever saw in my life was when Mrs. McGraw would write my name on the blackboard.

I rubbed my hand over the desk, and I felt all the cut places and scratches and marks that other children had put there. Some kids had carved their names and I couldn't understand why. I thought, *Why would anybody carve a beautiful desk like this? Why would they want to destroy something when it's so badly needed?*

Papa made Mrs. McGraw a cow bell and when she would ring the bell for recess or for us to come inside, the tone of it seemed to say, "Quietttt down, pleasssee." It was almost as if you could hear her words come through the ring. When no one responded to the bell, Mrs. McGraw had to get stern. "Sit up straight in your chair and listen," she'd say.

Mrs. McGraw would ring the cow bell for all of us to stand up and get in line. Then she would go in the front of the line and walk us all out the door and down the steps into the school ground. She left me sittin' in at my desk. She turned to me when she got ready to go outside and said, "Nellie, you stay right here, I'll be right back."

When she come back she knelt down in front of me and caught my hands and looked me straight in the eyes and said, "Sweetie, don't' worry. I will help you learn to read and get you caught up with the rest of the class." She was really sweet about it. I hadn't ever gone to school before, but my sisters had. I had always had that polio and wasn't able to walk until the Indian man healed me, and then I was ready to go to school. Mrs. McGraw knew I was far behind and it was necessary for me to get caught up with the other children so I wouldn't feel left out.

She worked for three days, maybe a week, teaching me A, B, and C. I felt the doors of heaven had just opened up to me because the thing I wanted the most was my education. I was going to learn to read and write.

Mrs. McGraw was everything I dreamed of in a teacher. She was loving and kind and understandable, and she did everything in her heart and soul to advance me in education. There was something about her.

Something about the way she moved about that reminded me of my own mother. But that was just because of her kindness and her goodness.

She would walk down the aisle while we were doing our lessons, and I would admire the boots she wore. I followed the laces up the front until they met the bottom of her black skirt. They were almost up to her knees. She would gracefully walk with her back straight, taking each step as if she'd planned it. I thought, *Oh, I would love a pair of high top boots like that. If I could just walk like Mrs. McGraw and walk with a proud step.*

I had a little prayer that somehow or another I could have a pair of boots like her and, sure enough, my prayer come true. The next time we went into Ashdown, Papa bought me the high-top boots. He only had thirty-seven cents and since the boots fit me and he didn't have any more money, the man said, "Mr. Morse, she can have the boots. They are my donation to Nellie." Papa counted out the money and laid it on the counter. Thirty-seven cents.

I kept my moccasins on until we returned home because I wanted to be by myself when I put my boots on. I didn't want nobody telling me how to put on my boots. I just loved them. They made me feel proud and real appreciated.

* * * * *

One day we were all havin' lunch inside the classroom and there was a boy that went to school there by the name of Johnny Sudds sittin' across from me. He was very rude and unruly. He was always picken' on the women folks or always pickin' on someone because he was bigger than the rest of the class. When I started to eat my lunch, I got out my duck egg and begin to peel it.

He said, "So you bring duck eggs to school?" And then he hollered out, "Nellie Morse brings duck eggs to school! Yak! Yak!" And all the other kids laughed.

Then he started out to calling me Duck Egg, and it got the other children to calling me Duck Egg. "Hi, Duck Egg," they'd say. I felt hurt to think that I had struggled so hard to get to school and somebody would be mean to me.

Then, I looked at Johnny one day, and I said, "So you don't eat duck eggs?"

"Oh, yes," he said. "Sometimes."

Then I asked him, "Well, where does your daddy get the duck eggs from? Do you know?"

"My daddy gets them from a man down the road," he said.

"That's Fred J. Morse where you're gettin' your duck eggs from and that's my daddy."

He kinda calmed down and hid his face and no longer bothered me after that. After I shut him up.

Later, when all the children went out the door for recess, Mrs. McGraw came back in to help me. She petted me on the shoulder and said, "I really appreciate what you did, for that boy has harassed the whole school."

* * * *

One morning, whenevern' I woke, the sun was shining over the mountain and through my window and I heard a clanking sound. It was the apple man coming. I heard his voice a-singing, "One a-apple, two a-apple, three a-apple sweet. Sweet apple sweet." He had tin cans with ropes tied on them, draggin' behind the buggy, and as the cans hit each other and made a sound you could hear him a mile away a-comin'. I left my room, went out on the front porch, and called out real loud to Papa, "The apple man is comin'! The apple man is comin'!"

Papa come in from the farm and went to the kitchen and gathered a basket of green and white duck eggs to trade the apple man for apples. He had a basket of eggs and five pennies, and we ran out to the buggy. The apple man had some big red apples and some yellow apples. I picked out the biggest and reddest apple there was and set it aside for Mrs. McGraw.

Before school started the next day, Mrs. McGraw was a little late, and I placed the big red apple on her desk. She hugged me and loved me and said, "Thank you for the apple. It's the prettiest one I've ever seen. You are my special pupil."

I thought she was talking about the pupil in my eyes, and I asked her.

She laughed and said, "You're my special *student*, Nellie, and I love you so very much."

Before I left school everyday she would hug me and say, "I love you, and you come back now, you hear?"

* * * *

One day Papa didn't show up after school, and it began to snow, rain, and sleet. We begin to walk home, and it was snowin' so hard you could hardly see your hand in front of your face. I had on two coats, and I taken one of my coats and wrapped my oldest sister Hattie in 'cause she was always so little and frail. I was always afraid of losing her. I put Edna in a big barrel off the side of the road so she would stay dry and out of the snow, and we listened for our daddy. I knowed he would come. I knowed that when we didn't show up at home, Papa would be there. I could always count on him. He was one of the best friends I ever had.

Everywhere was white with snow, and it was cold. So here come Papa in the wagon. He'd holler out, "Hattie, Hattie!" And then he would wait a few minutes, and he'd go to hollerin', "Nellie, Nellie, Nellie!" Just as loud as he could, comin' up that road with that team of horses and the wagon. So, finally, when I heard him, why I got out and waved him down. Everyone got in the springseat of the wagon, and he wrapped us in coats and blankets and we went back home.

It was so cold 'til it was freezin' the animals that were in the woods to death! Mr. Perry told Papa, "In all the years—near fifty years—I've never seen a worse snowstorm."

"I believe you're right," Papa said. "It will freeze our animals if they don't have shelter."

Papa took out the next mornin' to hunt up quail. I guess he found about twenty-five or thirty, nesting, and a bunch of eggs and things. He brought them back to the house and then took off to the woods to save more of the animals. He brought bags and bags of quail and doves and all kind of fowl and a possum or two. He begin to store them in our barn.

He taken toe sacks and heated them around the fire and laid the frozen birds and things on them to warm them up, and then laid more toe sacks over the top of the birds. Once they got warm they would fly to the top of the barn, trying to get away. But they didn't know how cold it was outside or they wouldn't have tried to get away. The weather was miserable.

1928 was the first year I got to go to school. That's what the records still shows. I went to school forty days up until the blizzard. The school shut down, and when they opened up in the spring, Papa had a barn full of animals. He made a stove to keep the animals and things warm and to keep us warm while we picked the peanuts off the vines.

And whenevern' the snow begin to melt, why, here come the game warden. He was a tall, big, old, rough-lookin' man, and his skin looked like an alligator's skin. He asked me, "Does Mr. Morse live here?"

I said, "Yes."

He says, "Well, I guess I'll have to take him to jail."

I said, "What for?"

He said, "He's got a lot of illegal quail and things out there in that barn."

I said, "Yes, he's saving their lives. Him and some of the other neighbors got down there in the woods and lowland flats to get the rabbits and coons and save everything they could 'cause everything was a-freezin' to death. It was a terrible blizzard."

He said, "Oh, so he was a savin' their lives!"

"Yes, sir. He don't intend to do nothin' wrong. We've eat a few rabbits along the way that was too cold to save, but yes, we've got plenty of them out there. You'll find him out there in the barn—probably feedin' the animals."

The game warden went out there to the barn and Papa invited him in. He seen what a good job Papa had done. He had a fire was going 'cause it was still pretty cold, and there was corn and peanuts and hay for the birds and the animals to eat.

He had the birds in the top, and the coon and the possums would crawl back in under the peanut vines to stay warm. The cottontail rabbits all huddled together, and the swamp rabbits hopped around all over the barn. They seem to understand that it was spring.

He give Papa a badge that day to wear as game warden for saving the animals. Of course, Papa was just like that. He always fixed everything. It just seemed like if something was wrong, he'd fix it.

Papa got money every month from then on as long as I can remember for being game warden. He got the first check, and it was really a blessing 'cause back then we only could have flour once a year and that was on Christmas. It was rare to have anything that come out of a store.

When it got a little bit warmer where the birds and things could survive, Papa turned them all loose.

It come spring of the year, and I went back to school. I felt so good to be back in school with the other children. I was more than rejoicing. Mrs. McGraw put her arms around me and hugged me and held me real close. She told me, "You're sick, honey, you're sick." I said, "Oh, no, Ma'm, I just feel a little bit bad. She put her hand on my head. "Your head is so hot I can't hold my hand on it, and you're going have to go home."

Whenevern' we got back to the house, I kept getting sicker and sicker. Papa went and got the doctor, old Dr. Ringo—the one that said I wasn't gonna live—and he said I had Malero Fever. Now days they call it the rheumatic fever. I was another four weeks in bed and after that, why school was out for the summer and different things happened. That was the last day of the forty days that I spent in school.

Mrs. McGraw really loved me, and she put every effort into teaching me how to read and write. She had learned me my ABCs, and how to sing the ABCs, and how to count to ten. I felt real grateful and thankful I had the opportunity to go to school for forty days.

Mrs. McGraw was my first school teacher, but not my last.

Chapter Nine
1929

The winters were hard there in Arkansas during the Depression. It was during Hoover's time, and he starved us all. He padded the rich folks' pockets and starved the poor people nearly to death.

We worked the year around preparing and storing food for the winter. There was a stairway off the side of the house that went down to the cellar where we stored our food. It was a large room with log walls sealed with mud. There was no lights down there—only a big candle Papa made out of beeswax that throwed off a real good sweet odor, like wildflowers. We would take lilac petals and make perfume out of them, and then we added that into the beeswax to make it smell like honeysuckle vines.

One corner of the cellar had cans of fruit and vegetables, and the other corner had a potato bed in it. We could have fresh Irish potatoes year round. We placed our cabbage and carrots in under a layer of dirt and hay, around the edges of the potato bin so they stayed fresh all winter. We had a big pine chest to store the sugar cured and smoked meat in—cuts of bacon, dressed-out ducks, and hams. We were lucky. There were people out there that didn't have nothin'. They were like the grasshopper and didn't save for the winter.

Papa was a very giving man, and he always stored enough for our family, and then he always put some away for the people that lived like grasshoppers that didn't put up the food for the winter. Papa would help them through the winter to keep them from starvin' to death. He helped people all around Little River County. From Richmond to Ashdown and up through Foreman. Papa would take large hams out of our meat locker and cut them in two, making sure that both families had the same. He give away corn, duck eggs by the hundred, and big bags of potatoes.

Papa also traded his work for food. He fixed pots and pans, sewing machines, and guns and would trade it for chickens or honey or things other people had that we didn't have. Times was hard. You didn't run to the store every time you needed something. You learned to do without or fix it on your own.

My daddy got up one morning and there was frost on the ground and it was cold. He said, "This is good weather for hog killin'. We're gonna have to get these hogs killed so we have meat through the winter." And so he taken the team and went out to get some help to kill the hogs. When Papa come back there was Berta Mae Nolan riding in the back end of the wagon with her feet hanging down, and her daughter Roberta, her son Bud, and a boy they called Brown. I don't know what his other name was, but they always called him Brown.

Rid'n' in the back end of the wagon there, Bud Nolan had on a pair of blue overalls and one of the suspenders was kinda off his shoulder. He was tall and thin and a colored man. I think he was about thirty-five years old at this time. They came with their mother to help with the hog killin'.

During the meantime, why Bud started to get out of the wagon, and his mother told him, "I have raised you to be decent and respectful. You get that suspender back on that shoulder, boy. And now! I don't want to catch it off no more!"

So, he did that, and he got out of the wagon and he sauntered over kinda where I was at and asked if he could help me build a fire around the washpot. I said, "We've got some pine splinters in our wood box up on the porch. If you'll go get 'em, it will help it to start a whole lot easier. It will catch on fire faster."

We built a fire around the two big washpots and got them rollin', and Papa went into the house and got a twenty-two shotgun and killed the hogs. I hid my face and stopped up my ears 'cause I didn't want to hear it.

We got the hogs all cleaned and dressed. Berta Mae, she helped with the cleanin' of the chitlins and savin' the blood to make blood pies out of, which we didn't eat—but her family did. It was really exciting!

Then we would take and put enough salt in the washpot with water to where you could dip a ham, or two hams at a time if you wanted to, and then we'd put a whole egg in. The egg would float if it had enough salt in it. We would dip the ham in while it was boilin' hot, and then we would hang it on a rack and let it dry. 'Course, it was durin' the winter and it was cold. There was a big old frost on the ground every mornin'.

Everyday, everyday, we worked. We'd put the season on the meat, which was sage, pepper, and salt, and then we'd roll the sausage in our hands after we got it worked up real good where the seasons were all in it. Sometimes there would be two of us rollin' out the sausage. Then that sausage would be taken and hung on a rack, or hung up on a tree limb and let dry.

Papa sugared-cured the hams and all the meat, and put it in a lock box. What we had back then was a meat box 'cause people didn't have refrigerators and ice boxes like they do today. We didn't know any different. We didn't know there was such things as ice boxes and refrigerators to keep your meat.

Whenevern' we got ready to eat it, we would slice off about a half-inch piece at a time, and it would leave a perfectly round patty. Then, we'd take and lay the patty in our skillet and fry it nice and brown until we had fresh pork sausage.

We got the sausage sugar-cured and put away with the help of Berta Mae and Bud. Bud was one of the most politest men at the time that I thought I'd ever seen. He called me "Lady Nellie." He was wonderful. He'd help his mother every time she'd say, "Bud, will you do this?" He'd say, "Yes, Ma'am!" He was right there, and he was so helpful. He taken the hog livers and put them in a dishpan and grabbed them and run and put 'em on the table for her and everything.

Of course, whenevern' they got ready to go home at night, Papa give 'em half of a hog liver and some pork sausage for helpin' us.

This whole scene happened there in Arkansas—in between Ashdown and Foreman. We killed two large hogs. Looking back, I guess they'd weigh at least three-hundred pound a piece. They were huge hogs. That meat would do us pretty well until way up through the following summer. Of course, we give a lot of it away to people that was hungry and people that needed things. My daddy was a giver, too—a mighty fine man.

He was a wonderful person to the whole neighborhood and the whole community. He would get out and go from house to house, or people would bring their washpots or their pans that had holes in them and he would solder the pans so people could use them to cook with.

After the hog killin' was over, we started workin' on the peanuts. We had raised a big field of peanuts. I learned how to pick the peanuts off the vine while I was at the orphanage.

Every night, why Papa would have to take Mrs. Nolan and Bud home with a load of stuff. Later, I got to where I could drive the wagon and team pretty good and I could take them home. Papa always fixed me a harness to set me on the springseat so I wouldn't fall off of it. He'd done that when I couldn't walk at all. I still used it even when I could walk because sometimes there'd be bumps or holes in the road and I'd slide around on the seat.

Towards the end of the peanuts, Berta Mae would come and help with the corn. We would all work together—maybe pick off peanuts one day and shell corn the next day. Oh, it was some of the prettiest yellah corn you ever seen! Papa made us some cornshellers out of a piece of stone pipe and a board. We'd rub the good parts off into a wash tub and the bad parts, why we would put them over in a bin for the hogs and the cows. We never wasted nothin'. Times was really hard. For people that just worked day labor on the farm, it was almost impossible when the farmin' was done, for 'em to live.

We all worked around there until way up in the spring. Berta Mae would help Papa wash our clothes or show us how to wash our clothes and help around the house. She even taught me how to make cracklin' cornbread and a lot of other things that I didn't know. And I still to this day, make what I call "Berta's Cornbread." She also taught me how to fry the sausage and meats and to put something over the top so that it wouldn't pop the grease all over the place. She taught us a lot a little nice things.

These colored people—Berta and Bud—were awfully kind. A lot of days, Bud Nolan, he would come and shuck the corn—enough to do us women folks two or three days of shellin'.

As time went on, why Berta Mae's cow had a little calf, and she told Papa once or twice a week she could give us some milk. "Nellie has been so sick and she is so run down," she told Papa. "She really needs some milk." Papa was real pleased with that.

My daddy would give her meat and stuff, and she would give us a gallon of buttermilk. It was awfully good and cold. She would keep it in the well until she had to go to work or something, and I could get it out myself.

Chapter Ten

One day there was a young man by the name of Cleo Parker that come to our house lookin' for steel traps from Papa. He was wantin' to put up a trap line and trap red fox, and somebody in town told him Papa does a lot of trappin' and that he might have an extra trap or two he could trade or sell. He was a fairly nice lookin' man. He was about as tall as I was and cross-eyed in one eye. His hair was a dark, black color and he combed it straight slick back.

Me and him got acquain'ted with each other, and he would meet me once a week on the trail across the creek. He'd help me across the foot log, a big tree that fell over the creek. He'd take my hand and steady me so I wouldn't fall off of the log, and when we got to the other side he'd take both hands to help me down on the ground.

He'd walk with me about a mile-and-a-half across the river bottoms to Berta Mae's house. She lived in a small white house on a big farm. He would wait across the road so nobody would see him with me, and I would go and get the buttermilk from the well. I'd give him the milk to carry until we got to seeing distance from my house, and then he would lean in toward my shoulder and give me a tender-loving hug, and I would take the milk and go on home. On my way home I would think, *Oh, how good he smells.* He wore Blue Night cologne and always left his odor on my clothes. Hattie and Edny would tease me about gettin' into men's cologne, but I would grin a little bit and go on. Nobody ever knew we was together. Week after week we did this.

The harvestin' of the corn had come, and everybody was working in the fields and things and this horrible thing happened at this particular time. I was going over to Berta Mae's house to get milk one day and was across the road from where they lived. Cleo wasn't walking with me. I heard an awful scream—a blood-curdling scream, "Don't do that, don't do me that way!" It wasn't long until I heard another scream, "Don't kill me, please, don't kill me!"

It reminded me of whenevern' I lived at the orphanage.

I was hid across the road from Mrs. Nolan's house behind a big, heavy bush. I squatted down there so I wouldn't be seen. I couldn't go and help whoever was screamin' 'cause I was afraid something would happen to me. After a few minutes, a man come walkin' real fast out of the back door and got on a big, red horse with a white-glaze face. Just as soon as he got on his horse and rode off in a hard run, I run as hard as I could to that house to see what had happened.

Roberta was laying on the floor in a puddle of blood. She was bloody all over. This man had raped her and beat her nearly to death. I guess he left her for dead because she wasn't breathing, and I couldn't get no results from her. She was unconscious on the floor. He had jerked the sheets off the bed and they were full of blood.

I fell down across her and I begin to hug her and pet her. "It's going to be alright. Come on, Roberta, we're gonna make it through this." I got some cold water and went to washing her and trying to bring her to. I begin to sing and hum, "When the roll is called up yonder, I'll be there."

Let us labor for the Master from the dawn till setting sun,
Let us talk of all His wondrous love and care;
Then when all of life is over, and our work on earth is done,
And the roll is called up yonder, I'll be there.

About that time, Bud Nolan and Brown shows up.

"What happened? What's happened to my dear sister?" Bud said. He fell down on the floor beside her and begin to question her. Her mouth was so swelled she could hardly talk above a whisper. He begin to rub her face with his hand. "Wake up, Sis. You've got to wake up! Tell me who's done this awful thing to you!"

Roberta tried to open her eyes, but they was beat shut. She was spittin' out blood and cryin' all at the same time. "He raped me. He raped me," she said twice in just barely above a whisper. "The white man, the farmer did this to me."

When she told Bud that this man had raped her and beat her nearly to death, he and Brown took off in a hard run. When they got to the gate at the back of the house, Brown reached down and picked up a poleax, and they took off towards the river bottoms. That was the last I seen of them for a while.

About that time, Berta Mae come in and she helped me get Roberta up on the bed. I told Berta Mae what I had heard and what I had seen and that Roberta had told Bud and Brown who did it. She said, "That lowdown dog. He left the field shortly after she did. They were all workin' in the field with the corn, and they let Roberta come home an hour early to fix lunch. Then this man come and did this to her."

One thing brought on another, and about three days later I started to tell Papa what had happened. But he wouldn't let me tell him. He taken his thumb and finger and put it together and touch one cheek and pull it across his mouth and until he got to the other side. This meant shut up and don't never mention it again.

Well, I couldn't tell Papa, and a few days later the sheriff come to our place with a bunch of dogs, a-huntin' Bud Nolan and Brown. I listened to see what was said. They said that the lowdown farmer boy, Bud Nolan, had killed this white farmer. I wanted to stand up and scream as loud as I could scream, *That man got what he had comin' to him. It doesn't matter what Bud had done. He couldn't have done enough to this white farmer to pay for the crime he had committed and what he'd done to poor little Roberta.*

That started it. They shut Mrs. Nolan off from the grocery store. She couldn't get bite of anything. They wouldn't sell her nothin' in the town of Richmond. Me and Papa made up our minds that we was going to see her through it. Bud had gone, and the dogs and the authorities was a-huntin' him, and they told Papa to be sure to keep us little girls in the house 'cause them boys was bad. There was no tellin' what they'd do to ya.

Bud and them thought they was doing what was right because of what that man had done to their sister. But, that part never did come out. It was always how lowdown and how rotten they was and how they had disturbed the whole countryside.

It went on, and finally the lakes and things begin to fill up with water from the winter snow and rain. One day Papa and us girls went and caught a lot of big fine fish over at Walnut Bayou. This one day, I won't never forget, we was out there gettin' the fish and the sheriff were out searchin' around the big lake for the poleax, or any evidence that would lead them to Bud Nolan and Brown. I was in the boat, and I looked up and seen the poleax in the fork of a tree. I didn't say anything. I just turned my head, hoping that the sheriff's department hadn't seen what I'd seen. We got the fish out and left back home.

Later on that day, Papa had taken us kids to church and some of Papa's friends from church come to our house to eat fish that night. Papa built a fire outside, and we had plenty of grease to fry the fish. The folks that come home with us had two little girls. It was moonlight, and it was really pretty and the girls wanted to play hide-and-go-seek. Papa and the man and woman sat on the front porch, and they could watch after us pretty close, playin' hide-and-seek.

One of the girls was counting for us, and I went and stepped into the henhouse 'cause I couldn't run very fast and couldn't get very far. When I stepped into the henhouse to be hid, Bud Nolan put his hand over my mouth and said, "Lady Nellie, don't scream. Please don't scream. You know I'm not going to hurt you. You know me. Now if I turn you loose, you're not goin' to tell nobody?"

I said, "No, I won't tell."

"Lady Nellie, I'm on the run."

He was trembling when he put his hand over my mouth because the law was after him, and he was afraid they would catch him there. He looked all beat and worn out from runnin'. His clothes were all dirty and raggedy, and his hair looked like he had an afro. It was standin' straight up. It made his head look twice as big as it originally was. He always kept his hair oiled down, but at this time it was standin' straight up because the heat and sun had dried it all out.

"Wait right here in the henhouse," I said to him. "There are some big pieces of fish as big as your hand that Papa fried up."

I got a can of black pepper, half a pound of corn bread, and two big pieces of that fish. I dashed out the back door and into the henhouse and handed it to him.

"Now you take this black pepper. You know my daddy, I've heard him say a lot of times that if you put black pepper on your shoes the dogs can't trail you."

Bud kind of patted me on the head, and I turned around and ran out the henhouse shoutin', "Ollie Ollie Oxen Free!"

That meant that I had got back to the base without getting caught.

It wasn't thirty minutes later, and here come the sheriff and all the dogs. They must have had ten dogs huntin' Bud Nolan. They had trailed him to our house. They'd picked up his scent about five miles from their mother's house, over on the other side of the bayou.

I would go over to Roberta's house and stay with her 'cause it was so scary for her. I knew that Bud wasn't gonna hurt me. I had no fear of that boy, or Brown, after knowing them as well as I had during the past. I knew they weren't gonna hurt me. When the sheriff picked Bud up, all of Little River County shut Berta Mae and her family off from sellin' her anything. I mean, she couldn't buy a piece of meat or a loaf of bread or nothin'.

And, so this one particular time I was ridin' our old mare, Nell, that was practically blind, and Papa fixed me two bags of corn. I had Berta Mae's bag on one side and ours on the other so it would hang level. Berta Mae would come to our place and shell the corn, then I'd take her half to the gristmill where they would grind the corn and make cornbread or cornmeal out of it. At this time, when I got to the gristmill, a man there asked me about the corn. He turned to me and asks, "Who is this corn was being ground for?"

I kept my mouth shut. I told him, "This is being ground for Fred J. Morse."

He said, "We will not grind no corn for the Nolans."

All the time I was there at the mill I heard about this awful thing that these two black boys had done. I would have given my right arm to say: *That man raped that little girl and beat her unconscious!* But I couldn't say nothin' 'cause my daddy had told me not to.

There were so many times I wanted to tell them people when they'd be down on Bud and talking bad about him: *You don't know the truth about it. You don't know how horrible it was. You don't know what all this man done before Bud and them done that to him.*

Whenevern' we got back home, I managed to get Berta Mae's corn mill in gallon buckets. I put her cornmeal and meat in there, and I would carry it to her. Of course, Cleo was helping me carry it over and back.

Time went on with Bud Nolan being on the loose and gettin' caught. Whenevern' it came time for Roberta's baby to be born Papa wanted to take Roberta something. We went over there to the Nolans' house and we carried her two squirrels and some cooking oil and some grease that had come off the hogs.

Papa said to me, "That is a little white baby."

I said, "Yes, sir. That sure is a little white baby." And, I started to tell Papa again, but Papa wouldn't let me.

He said, "If those city people hear about this baby they'll take it away from that girl, sure as a whirl."

So I got word from my school teacher, Mrs. McGraw. She said, "Nellie, you want to be real careful. That girl has had a little white baby, and the town is coming and taking the baby away from her on Saturday."

I come home and told Papa that I needed the wagon and team hooked up. He asked me why and I told him, "They're gonna take Berta's baby away from her Saturday."

Well, this here was Thursday evening, I'll never forget it.

He said, "Alright, you be up and ready to go by four o'clock in the morning, and I'll have that wagon settin' out here."

I taken the wagon and the team early the next morning. There was a beautiful half moon shinin'—so bright you could pick a pin off the ground. I heard the squeaks of the wheels and the mockingbirds a hummin' all around me. I was feeling nervous and afraid I'd get caught, but I was listenin' to every sound around—the birds and the squeaks of the wheels—and this helped me calm down, for I knowed I was getting my dear friends in to safety. I went up by Richmond and over by the old colored church to the Nolans' little farm house.

When Berta Mae seen me, she come runnin' out of the house. "I've been waiting for you, honey. I've been waiting for you! I knowed you'd see us through this! And I told Roberta that you would see us through it."

We put some blankets in the wagon and wrapped the baby real good and took off just as fast as the poor horses could walk. We drove and we drove. Berta Mae had a brother that lived over in Oklahoma out there on the Blacklands. So, we drove thirty miles, or farther, to Oklahoma.

Whenevern' we got close to Foreman I got real tired because of the polio and Berta Mae fixed me a bed in the back part of the wagon and she took over and drove. We had to ditch the town of Foreman because the people was as mad in Foreman about the white man getting killed as they were all over Little River County.

We drove Roberta and her baby to her brother's house, and it was a great rejoice! We saved that baby. Whenevern' I got back home the next morning, I hadn't been home two hours and here come the sheriff's department. They had misplaced the woman and baby. Well, Papa had done taught me enough that you just don't talk to those folks. You don't say nothin' to them. He turned around and looked at me and did his same old little number. He put his thumb and middle finger together and touched his right cheek and pulled it across the left, and whacked it off. That meant keep your mouth shut. I wasn't allowed to say nothin'. I wasn't even allowed to talk to my own daddy about it. He was afraid they'd come in and kill all of us. There was such a racism at that time. Bud was black, and they wouldn't take the word of a black man over a white man. If we spoke up for the colored people, why they would have considered us "nigger lovers." The fear for my life and the family was the fear that Papa had.

A few days went by, and they shipped Bud Nolan's body back. They had electrocuted him and nobody had never, ever knowed the truth, other than me about what really happened and what went on.

So many times I wanted to stand up and scream: *You don't know how horrible it was and what that man did to this girl!* And, then she had the little baby, and they was gonna tar and feather her and run her and her mama out of town and take the baby. But they didn't get that opportunity.

I went with Mrs. Nolan when she got Bud's body. I taken the team and took her to Ashdown to the depot and they pried the lid off the casket so she could identify him. His ears were just parched. It was an awful smell. They had him in an old square pine box with some sawdust in it with a piece of an old sheet in it. He had been dead four days, and it looked nasty. When they opened the casket he had on an old, faded-out blue pair of men's sleepers. It was tied around his waist with a rope. Of all things in the world for that woman to have to see.

She was shakin' and cryin' real hard and she told me through her tears, "If you ever do have any children, it don't matter what they get in to, Nellie. You be there. You be there. You have that much love in your soul."

So we buried Bud Nolan at a little colored cemetery about three miles out of Richmond. They wouldn't let them bury him there in Richmond or none of the town cemeteries. There was fifty to seventy-five colored families that was there.

Well, thank God, I've lived a long life, and I've lived a lot of it by her word. It doesn't matter what my kids got into, it wasn't 'cause I wanted them to, and I was always right there waiting for 'em.

If anyone ever wants to take the notion and look into this and find that I'm a-telling you the truth, you'll find word for word just what I've said. And the truth is—this is the first time in history, and this happened over eighty years ago, it's ever been told. But I felt like if they're gonna write my story, they might as well know about Bud Nolan and the things I went through durin' that time.

I thank God for lettin' me have the opportunity and strength, which it hurts still yet, to mention the fact that when people make such awful mistakes and do these horrible things—they have to pay for it. Of course, I hated terribly bad for Bud to be treated like he was. They should have given him a pretty penny or a wooden nickel, of course, that's the voice of the child. That's the way I felt then, and I still feel that way. I don't believe in wrong doings. I don't believe we ought to kill anybody, but that man shouldn't have done what he done to Roberta. It brought back memories to me of things that happened to me when I was in the orphanage. It broke my heart to see her like that, and I would have just loved to have screamed just as loud as I could scream, *You're dead sure wrong! You're doing the wrong thing to take Bud Nolan! He was only takin' up for his own flesh and blood.*

Sometimes we have to stand up for our own flesh and blood, even if they're wrong. But Roberta was not wrong. That white farmer knew that she had left that field to come home and prepare dinner. He knew that he would have one hour before anybody would know about it, 'cause he was the man over the big ranch that belonged to him. He thought he could do anything he wanted to do and get by with it. But, he didn't get by with it. Thank God.

I'm glad I got this off my shoulders. It's been there for a mighty long time. There was a lot more to go with it, but everything was the truth that I told you. You can check on the burnin' of Bud Nolan—the electrocution of him. All that's on record. But the part that ain't on record is that awful man raped that little girl—and her just fourteen years old. He caused her to have that baby.

That's all I'm going to say about that story. I've needed to put that in my book because it's been there all my life. I've tried to ditch it and dump it and forget it, but it's still there and I'm glad to get it off my shoulders and somebody else knows now. Anybody that reads my book will read this story. Thank God! And, thank you, Jesus, for giving me the strength and energy to put it on paper. This is the end of Bud Nolan. I hope when you read it that you'll understand it.

I never did finish tellin' Papa about what happened. Even forty years later, I mentioned it to Papa, and he said, "You shut that up right now. It's done and over with. Let it lay." He was still afraid for us. For the family. Afraid that something would boil up.

Article on Bud Nolan, Little River County Newspaper, 1930.

Chapter Eleven
1932-1933

Papa taught me real well how to shoot a gun and how to go fish. Of course, I was a little late on account of the polio until that Indian man cured me. Times was hard, and you barely saw anybody with meat unless they raised hogs, and most people wouldn't even mess with the hogs.

Long before I could walk a step I could shoot a gun. It was for me and my two sisters' protection because my dad was often gone to work. He would go and hunt and fish to bring in food and take food to the neighbors.

He was a gunsmith, and he fixed sewing machines and guns. We always had a little bit better of a living than others because my daddy was so smart to do these things. I have kind of taken after him.

Papa showed me how to trap a rabbit. We hid behind a tree until the rabbit came and went into the hollow log where its nest was. Papa had built a little fire at the end of the log so the smoke would go down into the log. The rabbit would go out the other end into the trap where the turnips was at for bait.

Papa made me a pouch so I could carry my .22 shells and a few turnips. He put the pouch on my back, kind of like a backpack, so I could have my hands to pull myself up with if I got down.

Cleo finally asked me to marry him. We had walked together to the Nolan's to get milk and we were part of the way home and I had to stop and rest. I was give out. I sat down on a log and he sat down beside me. He smelled so good and so clean. He used his shampoo on his hair before he came to see me and dusted himself with cologne. We set there for a while and he held my hand and twisted my fingers 'til they were numb. He was real nervous. We heard the coyote running through the woods and the crows squawking in wild pecan trees. He got off of the log and got down in front of me and he said, "Nellie, would you kiss me?"

And I said, me being shy, "Well, I'm not married to you."

"Well, Nellie, would you marry me?"

I smiled real big. "I have to ask my Papa."

I was thrilled to think that someone wanted me after being sick with the polio. I was afraid people would me reject over the fact that I had the polio.

I asked Papa if I could get married and he asked me, "Who in the world are you going to marry?"

"Cleo Parker."

"You don't even know him! What makes you think you could marry that boy?"

"He asked me to, Papa."

"Do you think you'd be happy?"

"I think I would, and I do know him, Papa. He's been carrying my milk for six months now. We have times that we meet each other and he carries the milk."

Papa got a little smile across his face, "I just wondered how you were carrying that milk, as weak as you are."

We got married on my sixteenth birthday on the doorsteps of a little Baptist church there in Ashdown. Cleo had caught two red fox and one silver fox and he sold their hides and that's what we got married on.

There was no work for him or for me in Richmond, so after we got married he moved me about forty-somethin' miles away from my daddy. There was work to be done, pickin' strawberries, in a little town by the name of Horatio.

Cleo's brother Leo, his twin, lived in Horatio, and he come to get us in his old Ford pickup truck. We moved into a tent with a dirt floor, a full-sized bed, a stove, a small table with two cane-bottom chairs, and a little mirror I'd hold in one hand while I'd brush my hair with the other hand. Our clothes was kept folded in a wooden apple box in the corner.

One day Leo come to visit. "I'm hungry," he said.

Cleo told me, "Nellie, why don't you fix Leo some breakfast? I've got to go on to work."

Well, he didn't go on to work. He set there and visited a little, while I fixed Leo some breakfast. I fixed him a pan of biscuits, fried potatoes, a couple of eggs, and a cup of coffee—which was a good breakfast back then. He ate his breakfast and then came and hugged me. "I sure thank you for that good breakfast, Nellie. Can I call you 'Sis'?"

"Yes, sir. You sure can," I told him.

He thanked me again. "Sister, that was the best breakfast I've had in a long time."

About that time, why Cleo got up out of his chair and walked over there and hit me so hard in the mouth until he knocked me backwards about four foot. Blood begin to gush out of my nose and out my mouth and everything. It was awful. Leo, he got a towel and put it over my mouth and head.

"You had no business hittin' Nellie like that. She didn't do a thing. If you wanted to hit somebody why didn't you hit me? I'm the one that ate the breakfast."

I went on to bed and cried all night long because I didn't know what to do. I was about forty miles from Papa, and I didn't think I could make it by walking. I began to pray, *Lord, send me somebody to help me. I need some help.*

Sure enough, the next morning my husband got up and got ready to go to work. He act like there hadn't been a thing in the world that happened—and my mouth was still all swelled up and bleeding.

I had done planned on leaving. If I was to get anywhere in the world, I was gettin' outta there and goin home to my daddy. My daddy had never even as much as spanked me and hardly ever scolded me about anything. I sure wasn't going to put up with this after all I'd been through in my earlier days. I gathered a few of my things and my fishing pole and walked to Little River. I thought on my way out I'd catch a mess of fish for dinner.

It wasn't but just a few minutes after I got there I caught a nice big catfish. There was a wagon and team and a man and woman drove up. There was a house between me and the river, and the woman got out of the wagon and went in the house—it was her sister's house. The man brought the team on down pretty close to the river so they could graze. After a while, I give him my fishing place 'cause there was other people there fishing, and he didn't have no place to get in. And I done had all the fish I needed.

It wasn't long until he said, "You know, I'm gonna need some water for my team before I leave here. I'm a goin' to a little place called Richmond to get some water."

I said, "Oh, I have a big number three washtub at my papa's, and it'll hold all the water you need. My daddy lives over there in Richmond, and I sure would like a ride."

They agreed for me to ride with them, and I sit in the back end of the wagon. As we were going along in the wagon I remember thinking, *The Lord really answers prayers. It don't matter where you are and who you are and how far down you've gone, He knows about it and He will answer it.*

These folks taken me to Richmond and whenevern' I got out of the wagon, Papa hugged me and kissed me and was glad to see me. He wanted to know why I come home. I told him, "He hit me and then he cursed me, Papa, and I'm afraid he'll come here looking for me."

Papa said, "No man is going to mistreat you around me. And, if you don't want to go back, you don't have to."

This is how I met Cleo Parker. I married him and only lived with him seventeen days. He was just real mean to me. He wanted to slap me, and I left him. But it was too late then. I was already pregnant with Louise Parker, my oldest daughter.

Chapter Notes:

I found the following information which helped continue an accurate time line of Nellie's life:

Bond for Marriage License: Cleo Parker to Nellie Morse, February 23, 1933, Little River County, Ashdown, Arkansas. The bond included a letter of consent written by Fred J. Morse

> Ashdown Ark
> 2/20 1933
> County Clerk Little River
> Ashdown Ark.
> Dear Sir
> will you please issue Marriage licence To Cleo Parker and my daughter Nellie Morse
> Yours Resp't
> Fred J Morse
> Ashdown ark
> R#2 Bx 74
> witness to signature:

April 22, 1930 census: Little River County, Arkansas

Chapter Twelve
1933

I went and the spent the winter of 1933 with Grandma Williams, but I had my oldest daughter, Louise, before I went. I wanted to take her my baby to show her, and she didn't want me to leave. Grandma was sixty-five years-old and was expectin' a baby boy by the name of Benjamin. People don't ordinarily have babies at sixty-five years old, but my grandma did.

When I got there she was swelled like a toad. She says, "You can't leave me, Nellie. The doctor told me I have the dropsy real bad and a tumor in my stomach that is going to bust wide open. He says I couldn't possibly be pregnant at my age."

Grandma was ordinarily a beautiful woman with tan, rosy-colored skin, but at this time she looked pale and sickly. She had pepper-colored hair she wore cut short just at the burl of her neck, and dark brown eyes set back in her head that showed her sickness. As I was a lookin' at Grandma beggin' me to stay with her, I couldn't have left her at all in that condition. I agreed to stay with her.

Grandma fought against being pregnant. She would say, "I am not pregnant. I've got a tumor, and it's going to have to be removed."

Grandpa and Grandma was living at Falk, Arkansas, in close to Blue River bottoms in an old wooden house that had a chimney fireplace.

Grandma would sit and hold Louise and rock her while I helped Grandpa with the housework, the milking of the cows, and feeding the chickens and feeding the stock.

I got up one morning and went to the kitchen to put on a pot of coffee for Grandma, and Grandpa and I heard a little squeaking sound coming from outside. I went over to the window and looked to see if I could find what was crying and saw the door of the pig pen down. I broke in a run out the door to the pen and found a little pig in a nest of hay. It was shivering all over and still wet from birth. I wrapped it up in my dress tail and put it close to the lower part of my stomach 'cause that's usually the warmest part of the body.

"The sow must of broke down the door and ran off to the river bottoms to have the rest of her pigs," Grandma said when I come in. "Get you a towel and dry the pig off real good and lay her there on the oven door so the heat will come down over her."

The pig was so weak and cold 'til it couldn't even move. She was the runt of the litter and no bigger than the palm of my hand. I called her Sally. She was a little Polan China pig and had a white stripe across the shoulders and back around the neck and down across the front feet. The rest of her was kind of a rusty-brown color. She had a little bit of fuzz all over, and after a few weeks her hair turned dark.

Grandma said, "That pig is weak. It's got to eat, Nellie. Get a bottle and light a roll of paper and put it down in the bottle. The heat from the paper will draw the milk from your breast."

After I got the bottle good and full of milk, I took an eyedropper and tried to feed the little pig, but she was too weak to take the milk, and it ran all over her belly and all over me, too. I kept trying to feed her with an eyedropper, but she wasn't strong enough to swallow. I would rub her little throat, but I didn't get no success, and the third day, Grandma told me, "Nellie, I think you're losing the little pig. Try giving it your breast."

So I did, and she latched on and nursed until her little tummy was round and full. From that day on this was the routine. She would root me on the ankle when she was hungry, and every time Louise wanted to nurse, the little pig wanted to nurse, too. So, I'd put Louise on my right breast, and Sally on the left.

After three months, Grandpa said to me one day, "Nellie, that pig has got to go. It's getting bigger by the day and the next thing you know that pig will take you down and nurse, whether you want it to or not."

At that time, Louise was just about a year old so I weaned them both at the same time. Grandpa caught Sally and set her up on the springseat beside him in the wagon and drove off over the hill and across the creek to where the Tysons lived. They wanted Sally as a little pet. It just broke my heart. I cried and cried and would love Louise up every time I wanted to cry. I never would go back to see Sally at the neighbors because it just hurt me so bad.

* * * * * *

Grandma always sat in her rocking chair. There wasn't but one rocking chair in the house, and it belonged to Grandma. She would sit there and smoke her little pipe and tell me stories about the past and how the Indians were mistreated and how they were in such a struggle to live.

Grandma was only four foot eleven inches tall, but when she talked, she roared like a lion. It was important that you stood real still and listened to what she had to stay.

She told me many things. She told me about the White Buffalo Woman and of her teachings, and how she taught the Indians how to make the peace pipe. They didn't know how she got here. They thought she was sent from the white father of heaven, which is Jesus I want you to know. He sent her, and we all believed He sent her.

They didn't know where she got all these messages from, but she had 'em. She taught the Indians how to live and where to live and how to live with each other. She wanted the Indians to make peace with the white man so no longer their meat would be killed out and destroyed—such as the buffalo. She brought much happiness and peace to the world. Even though she may not be recognized today by a lot of people, a few of us old ones understand her.

She understood so many things that the Indians didn't, and they believed in her, and thank God they did 'cause I'm here today to tell the story. I'm here today to tell of how we all survived the signing of the peace treaty, and to tell the world about some of the great Choctaw leaders that walked in front of us and led the way.

One of the Choctaw chiefs that led the way was Chief Pushmataha. He was a great-great uncle of mine. As head chief of the Choctaw nation in 1814, he carried the responsibility of the tribe. He had the respect of the Choctaw and the white man and kept the people together, providing a way for all mankind to live together in peace. Stonewall Jackson said that Pushmataha was the greatest Indian he ever knew about.

He had the knowledge to know what was in front of us and was a great warrior. He believed in the heavens and the earth, and his beliefs stood as strong as the red oak tree through many storms.

The peace between the Indians and the white man still stands strong today.

Pushmataha later appointed his nephew, my great-great grandfather, Chief Nitakechi, to take charge of part of the Choctaw tribe. Nitakechi was one of the first Indians that signed the peace treaty at Dancin' Rabbit Creek with the white man. Of course, the white man give him a white man's name, and that was Williams.

My grandfather spoke up and told my grandmother, "If it takes my life to help save America, or to save the Indian tribes and our meat and our ability to live, then let it be. I am going to sign the peace treaty."

So the great Choctaw chiefs and leaders got together at Dancin' Rabbit Creek and agreed to sign. They all sat in a circle and smoked the peace pipe and talked it over about signing the peace treaty. White man had moved in on us and was killin' us out by the thousands and killing our buffalo and starving us to death.

Chief Nitakechi, before he gets ready to sign, he left into the mountains to pray. When it come time for him to come down out of the mountains, a black widow spider bit him on the butt. He had to stay in the mountains for three days before he got well enough to ride the horse down to the peace table.

In the meantime, the white man decided they wanted Chief Nitakechi to have a white wife. They hunt up a woman; her skin was like velvet, my grandma said, and her eyes were absolutely blue. She was a beautiful woman. The white man thought she was a French lady.

I don't remember what her name was and I'm sad about that. I wish somebody would tell me. So many of the older ones are gone 'til I doubt if I'll ever find what her name was. They brought her in and she was offered to Grandfather Nitakechi in marriage. They presented her to him at the peace table, and he took her hand in marriage to make peace. They had a baby and they named him Ambrose.

Ambrose married Sarah Ann Honoll, and they had a baby boy by the name of John T. Williams, my grandfather.

My Great-Grandfather Ambrose Williams was later killed in the line of duty at Pine Bluff, Arkansas.

My Grandfather John T. Williams growed up and married Elizabeth Roberson. She was Choctaw Indian. The Robersons was so badly mistreated by the white people until they left the "sons" off their name. They dropped it so they would be thought of as white people. From Robersons—they dropped it down to Roberts. That's what Grandmother told me.

My Grandmother Elizabeth and my Grandfather John T. got married and had seven children between the two of them. My mother, Nannie Chandler Williams, was the sixth baby of John T. Williams.

Grandfather John T. Williams sent letter after letter to Washington, D.C., trying to get his Indian rights straightened out so he could hold onto his land. When he went back to D.C. they called him a white man. They denied him of being an Indian because he had seven children and it taken too much paperwork to give them all something. They shut him off and kicked him off his land.

None of us have never received a dime of what was promised to Granddad Nitakechi at the peace table. None of the family has ever received a dime or a piece of land. My mother received a cow, a calf, a bull, which I believe caused her death, and six chickens from the Indians.

I want to bring this on forward. I was born Nellie Morse through Nannie Chandler Williams and Fred J. Morse. My Papa was an Indian agent, and he come to see John T. Williams to sign him and his family up on his Indian rights. They became good friends, but more than that, Papa fell in love with John T's daughter, which was my mother, Nannie Chandler Williams, a beautiful Indian maiden.

After many visits they decided to get married. John T. did not want them to get married until Mama was eighteen years old. Between the two of them, Fred J. and Nannie, they planned to take the horses to the Red River, swim across, then that would put them over close to the courthouse in Paris, Texas, where they married. That morning the sun was coming out bright and warm, and they got married and were both so happy and hoping for a warm welcome from John T. Williams. When they got back, John T. Williams had a loaded shotgun waitin' on them. He was a tough man, and no one wanted to cross him. After a short period of time and many good talks, the sun set and they settled their difference, and John T. Williams agreed to allow Papa to be a part of his family.

My Grandmother Williams taught me not to tell nobody we were Indians, and never to tell my children they were Indians. I growed up with the fear of the way the Indians had been treated. However, I love my little Indian mother, and I'm proud today that I'm Indian. I can stand on the Bible today and say them words. I'm redbone Indian. My skin shows it and my bones shows it.

Years and years went by, and Grandmother Williams passed away. Everything that ever connected us with the Indians had been dropped. Nobody said one word about it—us being Indian. But we are Choctaw Indian, and I show it today, and I've got grandchildren that really show it. I've got some grandchildren and their hair is coal black, like Grandma Williams, and their skin is just as white as snow and smooth like velvet, like my mama's.

The things that we have today was created at that peace table. The beginning of what we have today—every slice of bread we eat today, every house we buy today, everywhere we live today, was created by the White Buffalo Woman that was sent from the heavens and at the peace table at Dancin' Rabbit Creek.

Thank you, Jesus, for giving me this opportunity to write this story. In Jesus name, amen.

* * * * *

Grandma was awful determined not to be pregnant. In the last couple of months she felt Benjamin moving around, but she thought that was just the tumor getting bigger. She'd say, "Oh, look, Nellie, look. This tumor is getting so big it's moving around. I'm scared it's gonna bust open and come out of there." She didn't acknowledge being pregnant until just hours before she had Benjamin. I had just had a baby myself, and I realized some things had to be done because Grandma was having a baby.

Grandpa had gone out in the wagon to get the doctor and bring him back. Grandma begin to have Benjamin. I patted the bed down with my hands and pushed the feathers aside to make a sink place to protect the mattress, and then I put newspaper down and a sheet over that. Then I taken two sheets, tying one on the right hand side and one on the left hand side of the bedposts for Grandma to hold onto while she bared down to have Benjamin.

When he came out he was as red as a pickled beat. Grandma told me to get both feet and take them in one hand and spank his butt so he'd cry. That's the truth. I cut and tied the navel cord, and by that time Grandpa had got there with the doctor. I don't remember the doctor's name, but he said I done everything just perfect.

Benjamin was a big fine fat healthy baby—weighed twelve pounds; almost as big as his mama. Grandma sure got a surprise. The doctor had told her all along she had a tumor and was too old to have a baby.

Chapter Notes

Words of Nellie: "Before writing this book, I was uncertain about my family line. I thought Nitakechi was buried in the Congressional Cemetery in D.C., but apparently it wasn't Nitakechi, it was Pushmataha, which is a great-great uncle of mine.

Since we've been working on this book the confusion isn't so bad. It's all cleared up now. However, I got these messages and words from my grandmother when I was anywhere from three-and-a-half to five years old.

Then, when I went to see her throughout the years she renewed it all for me. But I still didn't understand the whole truth about it until now."

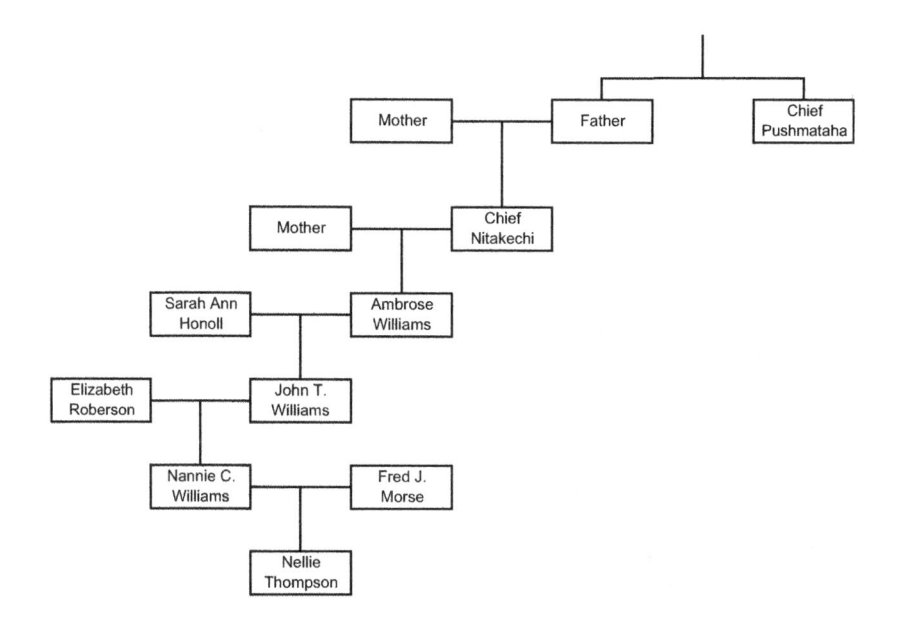

```
                                        ┌──────────┬─────────────┐
                           ┌─────────┬──┴───┐      │             │
                           │ Mother  │      │ Father│       │Chief       │
                           └────┬────┘      └───┬───┘       │Pushmataha  │
                                │               │           └────────────┘
                ┌─────────┬─────┴──┐   ┌────────┴──────┐
                │ Mother  │        │   │Chief Nitakechi│
                └────┬────┘        └─┬─┘
                     │               │
         ┌───────────┴──┐   ┌────────┴────┐
         │ Sarah Ann    │   │  Ambrose    │
         │   Honoll     │   │  Williams   │
         └──────┬───────┘   └──────┬──────┘
                │                  │
  ┌─────────────┴┐   ┌─────────────┴┐
  │  Elizabeth   │   │   John T.    │
  │  Roberson    │   │   Williams   │
  └──────┬───────┘   └──────┬───────┘
         │                  │
         └──────┬───────────┘
                │
      ┌─────────┴────┐     ┌────────────┐
      │  Nannie C.   │     │  Fred J.   │
      │  Williams    │─────│   Morse    │
      └──────┬───────┘     └─────┬──────┘
             │                   │
             └─────────┬─────────┘
                       │
              ┌────────┴─────┐
              │    Nellie    │
              │   Thompson   │
              └──────────────┘
```

1830 Choctaw Roll "Armstrong Roll" Introduction and Index by: Larry S. Watson, Published by:

Histree 1988 23011 Mouton Pkwy C-8

Laguna Hills, CA 92653

"It is interesting to note that Nitakechi was ill from a spider bite on the 22nd of September and was unable to attend the deliberations of the council. He undoubtedly had a major influence among his people and the tribe in general. He was continued as Chief of the Pushmataha District in the New Choctaw Nation until his death in 1845. He was one of the three tribal district chiefs who led the Choctaw people in the removal."

Official letter from John T. Williams to the Department of Interior: August 15th, 1909.

August 15th 1909
Valliant Okla.

Secretary of Interior
Washington. D.C.

My Dear

Hon Sir I am a Son of one of the signers of the treaty of 1830 Under Which this Choctaw Country Was given to the Choctaw nation of Red People and to thare Decendants

My fathers name Was Nittucachee I Was by the commission of the five civilized tribes tried to get my allotment in the Choctaw nation But Tams Bixby and Wm C Beall Lied me a of it So I am a Poor Indian I have no hon the - assistant attorney general. Hon J W Howell Can and Will give you the Whereabouts of my ca in full So Does the Reckords of your office Show it I am the man assembled all the ful Blooded Choctaw Indian to geather that had n allotment for mr Howell the atty general to Investigate there Claims Las november 1908 Mr Howell is acquainted with me if you Please further examine the Congressional Record of the sixtieth Congress first session Febuary 11th and on 1936 You therein see my case Laid open in full and I have all the Proofs in my Case that may be knealed before any Court and I Seece a coppy of the Decision of the United States Courts of appeals the other Day and The way Read and Understood That Decision That in Said court Provides that if a Indian mooves on a Piece of Land and Cleans it up and Lives on it is his

Know if I take up 30 or 40 acres and Clear it up and Live on it as my home Will you have me Put off it or Will you let me stay on it as I am verry old and not able to rent Land an satisfy the man in work that own Said Land a gain it is not Right for me to have to rent What is Justly mine and What I Bin Defrauded out af By mansfield memury + cornish et attorneys for the choctaw and chickasaw nations so they could it a little fee of ten Per cent to Beat me out of it Mr Sheretary I hope you answer this
   Your Obt Servant
    John T. Williams
     Valliant Okla.

Congressional Indexes, 1789-1969

Title: Response of Interior Department to request for report of J.W. Howell on claims against Choctaws and Chickasaws.

Sixtieth Congress first session, February 11th, 1908

I referred to the letter John T. Williams wrote to the Department of Interior and found the following index at the University of Utah library in February 2007. This information shows Nellie's line of lineage and relation to Ambrose Williams, or "Chief Nitakechi," one of the representatives of the Choctaw Nation who negotiated the Treaty of 1830.

1868   CONGRESSIONAL RECORD—HOUSE.   FEBRUARY 11,

CHILDREN OF SIGNERS OF TREATY OF 1830, UNDER WHICH GRANT WAS MADE, DENIED THEIR RIGHTS.

In other cases the children of the signers of the treaty of 1830, under which the grant was made, have been denied their rights, notwithstanding the fact that they have been residing in the Choctaw or Chickasaw Nation for the last twenty-five years, as is evidenced by the following official documents in the case of John T. Williams, a resident of Swink, Choctaw Nation, and who is the son of Ambrose Williams, who was one of the REPRESENTATIVES OF THE CHOCTAW NATION WHO NEGOTIATED THE TREATY OF 1830, AND WHOSE NAME APPEARS THEREON AS ONE OF THE SIGNERS OF THAT TREATY.

                         DEPARTMENT OF THE INTERIOR,
                             OFFICE OF INDIAN AFFAIRS,
                                 Washington, May 4, 1907.

JOHN T. WILLIAMS, Esq., *Swink, Ind. T.*

SIR: The Office is in receipt of three letters written by you, one addressed to the Attorney-General of the United States, one to the Department of the Interior, and one to this Office, relative to your enrollment as a citizen of the Choctaw Nation and saying that you are going to have your rights as a citizen before you quit, and that you are going to appeal to the Supreme Court of the United States.

In reply, the Office can only repeat what it has told you heretofore, that it has no jurisdiction to consider any citizenship matter since the 4th of March, 1907, and that there is now no authority of law for placing the name of any person on any of the rolls of the Five Civilized Tribes in the Indian Territory.

THERE WAS NO QUESTION IN YOUR CASE AS TO YOUR INDIAN BLOOD, AND IT WAS NOT DENIED BY THE COMMISSIONER TO THE FIVE CIVILIZED TRIBES THAT YOU WERE A PERSON OF INDIAN BLOOD. However, the possession of Indian blood was not enough under the law to justify your enrollment as a citizen of the Choctaw Nation. There are many persons of Indian blood who are not entitled to enrollment as citizens of the Five Civilized Tribes in the Indian Territory.

The Office has no reason to object to your appeal to the Supreme Court of the United States, if you so desire.

     Very respectfully,   C. F. LARRABEE,
                                        Acting Commissioner.

                     DEPARTMENT OF THE INTERIOR,
          COMMISSIONER TO THE FIVE CIVILIZED TRIBES.

In the matter of the application for the enrollment of John T. Williams et al. as citizens by blood of the Choctaw Nation.

                                 DECISION.

It appears from the record herein that application was duly made to the Commissioner to the Five Civilized Tribes for the enrollment of John T. Williams and his six minor children, Willis Jesse, Janie Virginia, Leona Gertrude, Johnnie David, Nannie Candler, and Jimmie Clarence Williams, as citizens by blood of the Choctaw Nation, within the time limited by the provisions of the act of Congress approved April 26, 1906 (34 Stats., 137).

The record in this case shows that John T. Williams was born about the year 1856 and is the son of AMBROSE WILLIAMS, AN ALLEGED ONE-HALF BLOOD CHOCTAW INDIAN, and Sarah Williams, a noncitizen white woman, and that the minor applicants herein are the children of said John T. Williams and E. C. Williams, a noncitizen.

Thirteenth Census of the United States: (April)1910 population, Oklahoma, Tishomingo, McCurtain County.

Williams, John T.(Head)

Williams, Elizabeth C.(Wife)

Williams, Leona(Daughter)

Williams, John D(Son).

Williams, Nannie C.(Daughter**Nellie's Mother)

Williams, Jimmy Clarence(Son)

Williams, Lieutishie(Daughter)

Martin, Don. Who was who among Southern Indians: "Nitakechi—Choctaw Chief, also called Fair Day, was chief of the Pushmataha District from 1828-1838 and again in the mid-1840s. He was the nephew of Pushmataha."

Chronicles of Oklahoma. Published by The Oklahoma Historical Society 1926 Volume IV, Oklahoma City, Oklahoma. "In the war of 1812, the Choctaws furnished a large regiment of soldiers to the American Army, commanded by Andrew Jackson. Their outstanding leader was a young man named Pushmataha."

History of the Choctaw, Chickasaw and Natchez Indians. By H.B. Cushman. Copyright, 1899, by H.B. Cushman. Greenville, Texas: Headlight Printing House, 1899. Edited by Angie Debo.

"Pushmataha, Apukshunnubbee and Moshbulatubbee were the head chiefs of the Choctaw nation in 1814, the latter being the youngest; but after the demise of the two former, Coleman Cole and Nitakechi, the nephew of the renowned Pushmataha, were chosen as their successors a few years previous to the treaty of 1830 at Dancing Rabbit Creek."

Treasury Department: Third Auditor's Office: November 27, 1886

--John T. Williams is the minor of Ambrose Williams

--Noted—13th Reg't Illinois Calvary. Ambrose killed July 10, 1964, while patrolling near Pine Bluff, Arkansas.

Chapter Thirteen
1934-1948

After Grandma had Benjamin and I got her back up on her feet, my daddy come and got me and baby Louise and took us back to Richmond. I was workin' with my daddy at the time in his little workshop, cuttin' out gunstocks, and things were looking up in the world. You could see the difference of the leaves on the trees and the cotton in the fields since [Franklin Delano] Roosevelt was put in.

I was working there in Papa's shop, and a man come in one morning to get his black walnut shotgun stock fixed. He was Papa's friend. "My daughter just got married," he said.

I told him, "I married, too, but I'm not with the man anymore."

He asked me, "Would you be interested in workin' for me?"

"I would, but I have a baby."

"That would be fine. I have a wife that could watch your baby while you work."

He had a laundry mat and a seamstress shop in Falk, Arkansas, twenty-five miles from where my daddy lived, which was fine, as long as he was good to me. He said he would give me a dollar a day and room and board. Well, grown men wouldn't get any more than a dollar a day, plus he was going to give me room and board and help with the baby.

I first started out sewing pockets in ripped places on people's clothing. I also did some dry cleaning and laundry for folks. I soon became good with the sewing machine, and Mr. Grubs asked me if I wanted to learn how to make men's clothes. He said he had a men's clothing shop next door and would like me to work in there. We went next door, and he showed me around his shop, and I met his wife who was crippled and in a wheelchair. I will never forget her wheelchair —it had wagon wheels on it, but it was comfortable for her.

I was workin' in Mr. Grub's store and my baby sister, Edny, called the last part of September 1934, wantin' to know if I wanted to go to West Texas with them to pull bolls of cotton. She told me she and her husband were moving there and she didn't know when they were going to be back. She said, "Hattie and Parker and baby Freddy are already in Texas, and Papa went with them. If you have any money and want to join us you could ride down with us."

I talked with Mr. Grubs, and he agreed that everything would be fine. As soon as I got to my sister's house, I put my things into Edny's car, and we headed to West Texas. We all knew there would be good work for us to do out there and that all three of us sisters would be together.

When we got there we found beautiful bolls of cotton. Fields and fields of white cotton just as far as your eyes could see. It reminded me of whenevern' I was a little girl and Papa sent Hattie to the cotton gin with a bale of cotton. Hattie took the money she got from the cotton seed and bought ten pound of candy instead of twenty-five pound of salt, like Papa had asked. Papa was really upset with her. He never sent her no more to the gins with nothin'. We had to trade duck eggs for salt from the neighbors during that fall and winter until spring come again.

When we got to my sister Hattie's house they were just sitting down inside the canvas tent to have dinner. Hattie made a big pan of cornbread and a pot of pinto beans. There was a young man sitting down at the table, and they introduced me to him. His name was Arther G. Bixler, but everyone called him Shorty because he was just over five foot, five inches tall. He was dark complected and had deep blue eyes and a beautiful smile. Shorty set across the table from me, and he smiled at me, and I smiled back. He was the most handsome man I believed I had ever seen. He had a small waistline and broad shoulders, and whenevern' he removed his hat when the food was blessed his dark hair laid across his forehead in curls.

The next morning we all got up with the sun. The man that owned the cotton expected all of us to be in the field when the sun came up, and we didn't leave the field until the sun went down. I braided my hair and wrapped it around the crown of my head and put a knitted cap over it so it wouldn't get tangled in the cotton burrs. I put on an old, long-sleeve blue shirt, one of Papa's shirts, and blue and white striped overalls. I wore old black tennis shoes, and I put the britches legs down in the shoes so the burrs wouldn't get into my feet.

The cotton was raised on rich black land and it was about waist-high. The rows was wide enough apart that we could get the cotton sacks down in the middle. The sacks were made of special cotton ducking fabric that would hold up to be drug on the ground. We put the sacks between our legs and the strap around our backs so we could easily throw the cotton into the bag as we went along.

The sacks would get so heavy you'd have to take your hands and catch the strap to pull the cotton sack. My back hurt so bad. If I hadn't been ashamed to cry, I would have broke down at times. But I would think of my daddy and how hard he had worked all of his life to raise us three girls, and it helped back the tears and brought a pleasant thought to my mind.

After the sacks were full, we would put them across our shoulders and dump them in the big trailer, then we'd go back to the fields to get another sack full. We did this all day long, from sun up to sun down.

Sometimes the sacks weighed ninety pounds per sack and other times they would weigh out heavier, a hundred and twenty-five pounds, or more. Shorty would tell me, "You sit here on my sack and I'll take your cotton up to the trailer and dump it, and then I will come back after my sack and take it and dump it."

I always thanked God that Shorty was there to help with my cotton sack because it was so heavy until it would strain every muscle in my body getting it over my shoulders.

We were each responsible to tend to several rows. Shorty and I were assigned rows right next to one another, side-by-side. That was Shorty's idea to keep me close to him. We worked hard and every now and again he would look over and say something to me, but I was bashful and hadn't been out it public very much.

We worked like this for about a month before we decided to talk to each other, or tell each other much of anything. He told me he had been in the military service and had been around, and he thought I had been kind of like a shut-in. I didn't tell him I had polio because this was a big secret. We started to visit more. He was about the kindest man I had ever met and was really good to me and good with my baby. This was something I had looked forward to.

It was hot and tiresome, workin' in the fields, but I was more than willing to do it to survive my family. Under the blisterin' sun of the cotton fields I dreamed of more opportunities for my baby than I had when I was a little girl. I dreamed of owning my own home and raising a big family. I dreamed of putting my children all through school because education was so important, even back then. My greatest dream was to have a home where we could set down and keep ourselves together. It was hot and tiresome work pickin' in the fields, but I knowed in my own way there would be better times a comin', and I would do everything in the world to make that possible. I wanted to leave the hard times behind and make it better for my baby than I had for myself.

Everybody was happy when the day was over. It seemed to be a rejoiceful time to get to be with baby Louise and to be at the campsite. My hands were all swelled and raw from the picking of the cotton because the cotton bolls were rough, and my back hurt me all the time. But I knowed I had to pick the cotton, and I knowed I had to make the money to support me and baby Louise.

Papa had purchased a tent, and me, Papa, and baby Louise slept in one tent, and Hattie and Parker slept in another tent. Edna and her husband, Howard Brown, moved back east to their home. They only stayed to work at the cotton fields for about three weeks.

One day it was kinda cold and windy, and I left Louise with Hattie, and me and Shorty walked to the little store down in Cone. When we got down to the store there was a man and woman that had just gotten married. The minister was there, and they were all so happy about it. We got our groceries and left. It was really cold and I walked ahead. Arthur caught up to me and he put his arms around me and asked me if I would marry him. "There is already a minister down there at the store, and he can do it, Nellie."

I smiled at him. "I would like that."

I was over rejoiced and was happy. When I said yes, he took me in his arms and kissed me and we caught hands and run just as fast as we could go to get back to the little grocery store.

Arthur asked the minister if he would marry us and how much it would cost, and the minister said, "I'll tell you what, I will pay for this if you will pay for the paperwork."

We proceeded with the wedding right there inside the grocery store. I got married in a pair of black pants and a blue work shirt, but I was as happy as if I had a wedding gown because I knew Shorty well enough to know that he was going to be good to me and my baby. The minister stood behind the counter and used it for a desk as he read from the Bible. The minister's wife stood near the minister behind the desk, and she was our witness.

Shorty didn't have a ring to put on my finger, and I didn't have a ring for him, either. The minister's wife said, "Just a minute," and she reached into her pocket and got out a handful of cigars. One of them had a plastic gold sticker around the wrapper. She offered it to Shorty to put on my finger. He was afraid he would tear the ring over my knuckle. "Give it back to me and I will put it on the lady's hand," she told him.

She put it on my hand, and we kind of smiled at each other, but I was serious enough that we went right along with the wedding as if it was a million-dollar gold band. After the wedding was over and we said our vows, we give the man five dollars, and he thanked us and wished us many happy years together. Shorty put his arm around my waist, and we walked down the doorstep smiling at each other.

Hattie didn't want to believe that we had gotten married. "You couldn't have gotten married because there wasn't a minister." I explained to her what happened, then Shorty come along and said, "I just married your sister."

"No, no, you couldn't have done that without somebody witnessing this."

"It was done at the station and a minister was there. Both the minister and his wife witnessed it," Shorty explained to her.

The following week, Hattie and her husband decided to go back to Avinger Village, Texas, because they had their own house and everything, down there. Papa also decided he wanted to join them. We took Papa to Lubbock so he could catch the bus back to Hattie's house.

The man that owned the cotton fields that we had been working on told Shorty he would pay us if we would stay there and help gather in the rest of the cotton. We agreed. We cleaned up the fields, then we loaded up all of our stuff into Shorty's old Essic and headed for Corpus Christi. He had been there before and worked on the shrimp boats, and we decided to go back and work so we could make a livin' for the family.

Along the way we stopped by a town called Three Rivers. Arthur had friends that lived there, and they were real proud to see us. They let us stay in their tent. We put the bedding down on the floor and went to sleep, and during the night someone stole Shorty's one and only pair of pants. He was a real dignified man and was embarrassed about it. A woman gave him a big towel to wrap himself in while we looked for the pants. We found his pants, but the money that was in one of the pockets was gone. This left us flat broke. The tires on our car had also been stolen.

The man we were staying with said he was going south and he would leave us his cardboard house, which was a little safer than the tent. It was barely big enough for a three-quarter bed for all three of us. We slept there for a day or two and then moved on to Corpus Christi and rented a place on Pismo Beach.

There was a man that lived next door to us that had a huge boat by the name of *Mrs. Betty*, and he was willing to rent it to us. Shorty stayed home with Louise because he spent eighteen years in the Navy and had all the water he wanted, while I was captain of *Mrs. Betty*. I would take her up to the Newasis River where the oyster beds was and collect oysters to sell to the market for money. Some of the oysters were so overly grown they were as big as my hand when they were shucked out of the shell.

Whenever the oyster season was over, we did the shrimp, and then we'd do the fish with gill nets. I got so good at it until I could stand on the bow of the boat and look out across the water and tell what breed of fish was nestin' in around the reefs. A lot of times it was red snapper or blue gill perch.

Times were hard back then. I was pregnant with my second baby and a cyclone came and blew all the water out of the bay. The rangers made everyone move because they thought Pismo Beach would be buried in water in just a few days or hours. We loaded up and headed back to Three Rivers. I had a baby girl, Ruth Irline, during this time. She was born on April 28, 1939. She was the most beautiful baby and had the most beautiful deep, blue eyes. She was little and tiny and weighed only about four-and-a-half pounds. By the time she began to dry up from birth, her hair begin to curl in soft, black curls. She was a little Indian baby, and that was for sure. Of course her daddy was full-blood Cherokee Indian. We stayed in Three Rivers for a while, and we fished and caught fish bait and sold them to the travelers and the fisherman. Times were getting harder and harder. Jobs were getting more difficult to find.

One day, Shorty left to get tested for disability. He'd spent eighteen years in the Navy, and he had gotten wounded, and that's what he drawed his disability off of. He took a bus up to San Antonio and went to the Veterans' Hospital there to be tested. They wrote him out a hundred dollar check. He went to the bank and had it all cashed in one-dollar bills. He brought it in a paper bag and threw it all over my bed. I was still in bed with the baby, not feeling too good. This was the most money I had ever seen. I asked him why he did this, and he told me he wanted me to see what one hundred, one-dollar bills looked liked.

"I brought home every penny and didn't take any out to even buy me a hamburger."

We spent the money on gettin' a car 'cause it was almost time to move again.

Chapter Fourteen

It wasn't long before work opened up in Tyler, Texas. It was in the summer time and the schools were all out. We were trying to find a place to live and work so Louise could go to school in the fall time. Louise was six years old, and my baby, Ruth, was almost crawling at this point. I desperately wanted to teach my children how to read and write, but I didn't know how myself. I wanted a better life for my children than I'd had for myself.

We had our old car (a Ford Model A); these were popular back then. Arthur would get out there and crank the motor to start the car. He would twist on that thing until the skin from his hands was about to wear off. He turned to me one day and told me he couldn't start it himself and to get in the car and put my foot on the brake, then when the car started, to put my foot on the clutch. We worked on it until the sweat was running off his brow. Suddenly, the car started, and I put my foot on the clutch, but instead I took my foot off the brake, and the car jumped the gully and went into a ditch in front of us. It scared me so bad I thought I would never drive a car again. My husband ran over and got me out of the car and pulled the car out of the ditch with some boards.

We picked berries in Tyler, and then left to go live in Greenville, Texas, where Shorty worked in a produce company, moving produce in a wheelbarrow. I went to a school and enrolled Louise, but we didn't stay in Greenville long enough for her to actually go to school.

Shorty came in from working one day and told me there was a place in town that was going to issue drivers licenses to women. He told me I should go and get one just in case something ever happened to him.

It was a beautiful day. I got all dressed up and was the first one in line to get my license. I was shaking all over and knew it was going to be the worse day of my life. I finally got to the front of the line and the man asked, "Why in the world would you want to take a man's place and learn how to drive?"

I told him, "It's something that I think is necessary to do."

He said, "Okay, but I'm only going to give you one chance and one chance only. You get in the driver's seat and I'll get in on the other side."

Shorty showed me all the driving signals. He told me, "No matter what the man says, you do it and you'll pass." When it was over, why, he told me I was about as good a driver as he was going to find.

My sister Hattie was in Lubbock, Texas, now and she wrote us a letter and told us the cotton was good and the weather was good and that we should come on out. When we were about a hundred and fifty miles from Lubbock, out in the plains, we saw this man and woman and their four kids stranded. The man thumbed us down and asked my husband if he could give him a pull to the closest station. Shorty, being the good guy that he is, told him he would be happy to help. Shorty asked him if his car would start and the man responded that it just wouldn't start.

So, we pulled the man's car about a hundred and fifty miles into a filling station. We were surrounded by beautiful fields of cotton. It was a beautiful area. My husband asked the attendant to look at the car, and he agreed that he would. The attendant opened the hood and told us he couldn't fix the car. When we asked "why?" he said, "The car doesn't have a motor." We turned to the man we had been helping, and the attendant asked him what was going on. The man told us he didn't think we would help him if we knew he didn't have a motor in his car.

Just when everything started getting real intense, a man drove up to the service station and asked all of us if we were interested in working in his cotton fields. He said he had a house and some tents we could stay in if we needed while we worked. Shorty told him we were on our way to Lubbock and that we weren't interested. But the man we had just pulled *was* interested. The blessing for this man was a job and a place to live. We never saw this man again.

From then on, every time we saw someone on the side of the road, we joked that his car probably didn't have an engine. We always had such a great time together. Shorty liked to say, "Live everyday like it's going to be the last one." The way we raised our children was to live everyday like there wasn't going to be another. And, it seemed to have worked. This story became one of our family favorites, and we laughed and talked about the car without an engine for quite some time.

When we got to my sister's house, we told her family about pulling this man's car for a hundred and fifty miles and it didn't have an engine! Hattie told us it was a great thing we had done, and no wonder it wasn't a very heavy car to pull. My sister and her family had already found a place to live. We found someone that had a place for us to live and work for us to do. The man told Shorty that he needed help with his windmill. And I spent time cleaning their house out.

One night, a cold blizzard came in. The trees hit us and the cold wind hit us. The icicles hanging down from the windmill were anywhere from ten to fifteen feet long. I'd never seen so much ice in my life. When the blizzard blew over, and the weather became better Shorty climbed up the windmill to get the icicles. We had to break the icicles and melt them in a pan and use them for water until he fixed the windmill and the water started to pump.

We all enjoyed one another and did a lot of church-going. We found a Four Square Church to attend while we were out there. Hattie asked me if I really believed in that stuff. I told her I believed in anything that believes in God. I don't care what it is, where it is, and how it happened. When people are praising God, they are praising Him in my name.

One day while we were at church a man approached my husband and asked him if he would like to do some farming. Shorty told him it had been a while since he had farmed, but as long as he could make a living for his family then he would do it. We picked up everything we had and moved to the farm. Life was good on the farm. We had another baby together and named him George. He weighed eleven and three-quarter pounds. A big, fine, red-headed baby. Hair just as red and curly as it could be. It was one great blessing for us to have a boy because there was so many of the women in front of me that had their babies, and they were all girls. He was a big baby until he killed my shoulders to carry him around. By this time, Louise was nine years old and Ruth was three. I enrolled

Louise in school for a few months there while we farmed the crops, and then after the fields were all gathered, we moved to another farmhouse way out in the country.

We worked the crops, raised a lot of peanuts, and raised two hogs. We also had some chickens and a rooster to take care of. I remember one Christmas Eve morning, two years later, I went down and put some hooks and lines into the river in hopes of catching some fish for Christmas dinner. We ended up having twenty-seven people over for dinner. I was pregnant and as big as a barrel. By the end of the evening the sun went down, and I was in labor until the next day—Christmas Day. Papa stayed with me, and Shorty went to go and call on a doctor. Papa told me we were going to have a Christmas baby, and sure enough, Sue was born straight up at 12:00 noon, Christmas Day, 1946. She was a big, fat, beautiful baby. We called her Nannie Sue. She was my fourth baby, and by that time, moving around from town to town, I was tired.

We stayed there about three years. This is the longest we stayed anywhere since I had been married to Shorty. He was always talkin' about moving. Louise and Ruth got to go to school for a little while there, but they never had the chance to catch up with the other children. At this point Louise was twelve years old, and Ruth was about eight. They had been in and out of school and were so far behind, and Shorty wanted to go back to Corpus Christi so we could work in the shrimp boats again. We had worked the fields in Lubbock and done everything we could do to make a living.

I was tired of movin' and draggin' the children from one place to another, just trying to survive. I knew that Louise and Ruth was missing out on all their schooling, and I was desperate for them to go to school. I had always believed an education was the most wonderful thing that could happen. It wasn't only me that was tired of moving, Shorty was, too. But this is how it was in Texas. We weren't the only people that was driving from pillar to post trying to get work and put food on the table. There were hundreds of families on the road, workin' at anything they could do to make a livin', but I knew there was better opportunities somewhere.

Down in Corpus we started a fishing business, catching and selling fish. One day I met a woman that lived upstairs from us, and her children had a beautiful education and could read and write. When I would see her children reading their school books, I would think, *Oh, Lord, if only my children could just get an education.* It made me think that we couldn't go on going from place to place and denying the children a chance to go to school.

I knew then I had to do more than I had already done—that my children couldn't go on like this, that there had to be some changes made. My great dream was always to educate my children because I didn't have an education and that was a great star in my brain that my children wouldn't have to travel around like I had to, to make a livin'.

One day I asked this woman, "How in the world are your kids so smart?"

She told me, "They went to school in Modesto, California. We used to live there, and it's nothing like living here in Texas." She said how much she loved California. "They make the kids go to school out in California. They furnish them a book, a pencil, paper, and they teach them." She said the jobs were plentiful too. "There are field jobs and canneries and all other kinds of work that a person could do to make a good living."

We continued talking, and after a while I decided I wanted to go to Modesto because I felt it was the right thing to do. I knew I had to talk to Shorty and ask him if we could move to California.

Chapter Fifteen
July 1948

I talked to Shorty. "I don't want our children growin' up like I did, not knowing how to read and write." I told him what the woman had told me, all about the schools in Modesto. "They'd give our children books and other supplies so they could learn to read and write. There are all kinds of jobs that we could work and make a good livin' at. The very bottom line is, I'm tired of moving about and not staying in one place long enough to educate the children or get them established in school. I want some place where I could settle down and call home with my family."

Shorty said, "You're dreamin'. It ain't like that in Modesto."

I begged him. "It's so difficult to move from place to place and get the children ready for school. Then we pick up and move again."

He said, "Nellie, I'm not going to California, and neither are you. You're just having a daydream."

For the next three days and nights I prayed to the Lord. I asked him to help me find a way to get to California so my children could be educated. It was a critical time in their lives to be educated, and I intended to see them through. Louise was fifteen, Ruth was eight, George was comin' up five, and then I had baby Sue that was seventeen months old. They were growing older everyday, and I knowed they had to have an education to make it.

I continued to beg and plead with Shorty, but he dug his heels in the ground and said, "I'm not going, the children are not going, and you're not going, either. So, forget it. Just forget it." He was real rude, and he meant business. But I meant business, too, and I was determined that my children were going to get an education, come hell or high water.

A few days later, Shorty went into town to the store to get some washing powders and coffee. It was about a mile-and-a-half into Three Rivers, so it would take him a while to get there. After he left, I packed my things and was gone. Me and my four kids went along the side of the little dirt road that led to the highway and only waited a few minutes before a big semi-truck came and stopped right in front of where we were standing. I opened the door to the truck, and the driver asked us where we were headed.

"To California," I told him.

"Lady, you have more nerve than I've ever had, hitch-hiking with four children to California."

We climbed into the big semi-truck, and he put the children in the sleeper part of it and made them all comfortable. I looked out the window, and I thought leaving Shorty was the worst thing I could have done, but he would not give in, and it had to be done. We had to come to California. The spirits were leading me to Modesto. To leave him was hard because he had been so good to me and the children, but it was the thing to do. The road in front of us looked long and hard, but I knew God was on my side. I knew He was with me and that He was watching over me and my children.

When we got to San Antonio, the driver helped us down off of the truck and he gave my children enough money to buy an ice cream and some dinner. This was a great blessin'. It made me feel like I was really doing what was right to make the trip. When we were at the station our truck driver talked to another truck driver and that took us to Tucson, Arizona, near nine hundred miles away.

There was town after town that we rode with that truck driver. We passed a lot of cactus and a lot of desert land. Finally the man got so tired, he said, "Nellie, I've got to pull over and get an hour or two of rest." He got his bedroll out and laid it under the shade of a tree near the road and slept probably four hours. While he was a-sleepin', I thought back on Shorty and knew that he would've tried to stop me and keep me from coming on to Modesto, but I was determined to get there.

When we got to Tucson, the truck driver bought us a motel room and dinner. We stayed at the motel until about one o'clock the next day, and a woman at the filling station came and told me she had found us a ride all the way on into Phoenix. This was another great blessin'. All through the journey, I could feel the presence of God. That He was watching over me and the children.

The woman and man drove us to the area where there was a bunch of cabins. The cabin we stayed in was right next door to the people that drove us there. She said it costs two dollars a night to live there and she could help me find work. She asked me if I worked, and I said I did and that the Lord was going to take care of me and my babies. She helped me get a job, and I started peeling potatoes and packaging lettuce.

Arizona was so miserably hot, but I kept workin' because I knew I needed to support my children. Truckloads of vegetables came in, and I worked in the fields in the morning picking up potatoes, and then I worked on the conveyor belt in the afternoon. I was working hard, and it was hot and my feet were blistered. I looked back on Shorty and I knowed he could make it without me. I knew he would be furious and would try makin' me go back to Texas if he ever caught up to me.

I worked here about six weeks then went next door and asked the lady how far away twenty dollars would take me. I gathered my kids, put our things in some cotton picking sacks, and she drove us as far as she could with twenty dollars and let us out at the edge of the Mohave Desert at a filling station.

It was late in the afternoon, and there was a man at the station with a brand new, powder blue car. He pulled over and asked us if we wanted a ride. He said, "You know you're getting ready to go across the Mohave Desert?"

"I didn't know this," I told him.

"I'm going across the desert and can give you a ride."

Me and the kids got in the car without saying anything. We got used to saddling up in silence.

There were several guns inside the car in the backseat. The man turned to me and said, "Tell the kids not to touch anything. Those are mine."

We crossed that desert without saying anything. It was really quiet in that car. I was scared. I was scared for my babies. With every breath I drawed, I was praying to God to keep us safe. I understood that we was in danger to even be in that man's car. I felt uneasy about it so I kept praying, *Lord, see us through it.* Then I thought of Shorty. I thought, *If he was here he wouldn't let this man hurt me and my babies.* But Shorty wasn't there, and I had to take all the responsibility on my shoulders. The word of prayer was the only thing that I had to keep us safe.

When we got across the desert and came to the border of California, the man turned to me. "I need you to do something for me. Pretend we are a family. When we get to the border, you need to convince the man at the station we are a unit."

A few miles down the road, when we got to the station, I turned to this man driving the car and said, "Honey, could you please ask where we could get some water for the kids. They are real thirsty."

The attendant at the station told us there was a motel about two blocks away and we could rest and get some water there. Although it was hot going across that desert, I was more scared than hot. I just kept praying to the Lord that this man wasn't going to hurt us. And, sure enough we were fine. The man paid a night for us at the motel and gave us some money to buy food. He thanked me and told me I did exactly right.

The lady at the motel showed us where a restroom was and gave me some soap and towels and showed us where to get something to eat. We sat and ate our food and then the waitress came over and asked me where we were headed. I told her we needed to get to Modesto. She told me she would help us get a ride, and she did. She talked to the next person that came through. I felt like God was guiding the trip; He was the one that was seeing us through it.

We got in the car with a man and he seemed real nice. He gave the kids some warm blankets to wrap up in because after you leave the desert it seems to get cold at night. We drove all night long until we got to Bakersfield. This man bought our breakfast and then said he was going to leave us here, but that he would try to help us find a ride.

He helped us find another ride, and this man took us to a place north of Modesto called the Log Cabin Motel. It was night now, and he tried to get us a room, but all the rooms were filled. I told him we would just find a place across the road behind some bushes.

I took all four of the children, and we went across the road and over the railroad track. We were tired and wore out and had just traveled over eighteen-hundred miles hitchhiking. I felt sorry for Louise than I did any of my children 'cause she had to help me carry the baby all along the trip.

We fixed our blanket and we all rolled up together in the dark. When I was drifting off to sleep I looked back on what Mama and Papa had said about educating us girls. Papa told Mama, "We need to leave these mountains and go back to civilization to give these children an opportunity to get an education." I thought, *Mama would be so proud of me that I had made my own stand and put my foot forward to getting my children an education.*

The next morning there was a train that come through, blowing its horn and woke us all up. I stood up and I looked over a huge orchard all covered in nice, ripe, juicy peaches. I threw my hands into the air and said, *Praise God! We finally made it to California! Now my children can learn to read and write!*

Chapter Sixteen
1948-1949

The sun was just comin' over the mountains openin' up for the summer day, and the fragrance of ripe peaches filled the air. I hugged my children and held them close. I told them that this trip wasn't hard on just one of us; it was hard on all five of us. Baby Sue was tired and cryin', and George's little red curls were just standing all over his head. Ruth's hair was so tangled until I had to get water to brush her hair with. Louise was give out from helping me with the baby and all of our feet was blistered from the long journey, but we was happy. The children was happy, and I was happy, too. Ruth was the one that spoke up and said, "Oh, Mama, I know we're going to make it. We're going to school."

We went across to the Log Cabin Motel and the lady that was managing the motel fed us hot pancakes and a glass of cold milk a piece. Just as we was finishing our breakfast a man came out of another cabin and had overheard us talking about finding a place to stay. He spoke up and said, "There are some empty cabins in Salida at Snow's Camp, and I've got to go near there to get gas, and I will give you all a ride if you want me to." I thanked him and begin to pray that we would find us a good place to stay.

He dropped us off at the filling station in Salida, and I asked someone directions to Snow's Camp. One of the gas attendants spoke up and said, "My sister might could put you up at her house."

This gas attendant was William Riddle. He marched hisself over toward me, and the cologne he had on was so strong until it almost knocked me down. He was a tall and thin man with dark curly hair combed straight back so it laid in waves away from his face. His eyes were a real clear blue, and when he looked at me he lit up like a Christmas Tree. He begin to talk to me about a place to stay and then he said, "Let me tell the man here at the station that I'll be right back, and I'll go get my sister Ethel."

Ethel Hillman was half-French and half-Cherokee and had long, blonde hair that looked like silk in the sunshine. When she talked her eyes lit up her whole face. She told me that she was about ready to lose her place if she didn't come up with the mortgage. She had been paying seven years on it, and they were gonna foreclose it in the morning. I said, "Lady, how much is the mortgage?"

She said, "Twenty-five dollars."

"Well, you must have just looked in my pocket because that's exactly what I have."

Me and the children gathered our things and walked to Ethel's house. I felt she was about the kindest woman I had met. She was really willing to lend me a helping hand, and at the same time I handed her a helping hand.

Ethel's house was an old ranch house and was painted white with blue trim. It was a very attractive place. It had about four big eucalyptus trees in front for shade, and to the west of the house was a big grape orchard, and the vines were hanging full of rose-colored and green grapes. Inside, the walls were white and all the fixtures stood out with colors. The floors were a beautiful hard wood. Ethel had scrubbed them until they shined like a new nickel. The furniture was old ranch house furniture, and Ethel wasn't afraid for the children to be in and around it because it was so old.

She told me, "We'll all cook and eat together until we have this all straightened out and you get you a place." I hugged her and thought this sounded wonderful. She gave us one big room to sleep in, and the other room was for her two children.

Ethel asked, "Nellie, how are you for working?"

"I will work for anything. I don't care if I have to clean up after chickens."

Ethel got up early the next morning and said she was going to work at the Manteca Cannery. She asked if I wanted to go. I was tired and sore from that long trip, but I wanted to go.

The cannery was a long, sand-colored building, and you could tell it had been there for many years. The air outside smelled like ripe tomatoes and ripe peaches. A smell that made me think of being on the farm with my Papa and sisters.

There was a long line of women standing inside waiting for jobs. The lady in charge came out from off of the belts and looked over everybody in line and pointed me out. "Have you ever worked in tomatoes before?"

"Yes, Ma'am, I sure have," I told her.

"Well, you come on up here and let's get going."

People were looking at me to see what I had done, which I hadn't done anything. I was the first person hired, and I hadn't been in California much over ten hours.

She got right beside me and went to skinning a hot tomato, and I went to doing the same thing. She asked me, "How long you been working in tomatoes?"

"Four or five years in my own kitchen."

"You really know how it's done."

I looked back on my Papa—to the things he had taught me. He had taught me how to can the tomatoes at home in a tin can and in glass fruit jars. It reminded me that the long hard winter was behind me and things was going to be better from here on out.

Later that summer, the last day of August to be exact, I enrolled Louise, Ruth, and George at Salida Elementary School. I had to take a day off of work at the cannery to enroll them. We got up early that morning, and the children put on their new clothes and their new shoes, and we walked hand-in-hand from Ethel's house to the schoolhouse. Louise and Ruth and George was all huggin' each other. It was such a beautiful sight to see my children going to school. Louise was fifteen, and she could print her name and could read a few words. Ruth could barely print her name and read very little, and George had never been to school because he wasn't old enough. It was a great day whenever I got the children all in school.

When the children returned that day, they all come running in the house, shoutin', "Look, Mama, we've got our very own school book!"

Ruth said, "Mama, I wrote my own name on my paper!"

I was so happy I broke down in tears to think we had come that far, miles and miles through the desert and through the countryside. We shared the memory with each other. Our struggles for survival will always be in my memory but so will the enjoyment and happiness of them getting an education and a better life that I had promised them from the beginning.

Time went on, and the kids were all in school and doin' good. I was awfully proud of my children. I loved them to death. I told them to love each other everyday like it's the last day of their life and we'll all get along. Sure enough, we had a little meetin' every Thursday night, and if one had done the other one dirty, or somethin' had happened, why we would sit around and visit. Of course, back then we didn't know what it was to have a TV or nothin'. Not even a radio. It was hard, but we made it! It was much better than it had been in Texas. Just so much easier until I just felt like we were living in glory!

Finally, after a few months, Shorty showed up at Ethel's front door. The children all run to greet him and show him their new school books. He was over rejoiced with them and loved them all up. He said, "Nellie, you really meant business when you said you was going to California to educate the children."

"That's right. I intend to give these children an education."

He hung around three or four days, lookin' for work and then come to me and said, "Honey, I've got a job in Buckeye, Arizona, workin' on the granary. I get some good wages there; better wages than I've had anywhere. If you don't care, I'll go back there and go to work. I will send money for you and the children until I can come home. Now, when the grain season is over, I'm comin' home."

"That's fine with me," I told him.

So, sure enough, about three weeks later, here come the sheriff. My heart fell to my hands 'cause I immediately felt like there was something wrong. He said to me, "Mrs. Bixler, you need to sit down."

I told him, "I ain't never found nothin' yet I couldn't take standing up."

He went ahead, "Well, three days ago, on August 21, 1949, Mr. Bixler fell to his death, and we've been huntin' for you ever since. Your address and phone number are the only ones he had in his purse. I came to tell you that you have lost a husband."

I felt my heart fall to my feet. I felt very sad about it and very uncomfortable. In fact, the minute that the sheriff left, I fell across the bed and cried 'til I couldn't cry no more. I loved Shorty. There wasn't any doubt in my mind that I loved him.

Him dyin' took a part of me away that I would never have again and brought back memories of my mother and the struggle I had to get over her death, and now I had to go through it again with his death. It was a tragic loss. I missed the love and the warmth and the tenderness of my dear mother. I just wanted my dear mother to hold me and hold me close.

Fred J. Morse, Nannie Chandler Williams, Nellie Morse

Uncle Clarence, Fred J. Morse.

Nellie, Hattie, Edna

109

Nellie's Schoolhouse in Foreman, Arkansas (photo taken on April 26, 2006 while the school was under renovation)

Nellie showing off a mess of fish she caught

Nellie Bixler, Arthur G. Bixler

Louise, Ruth, George, and Sue, two years after arrival to California

111

Back Row: Nellie, Edna, Edna's daughters
Front Row: Ruth, George, Sue

Fred J. Morse

Fred J. Morse

Edna, Nellie, Hattie

Nellie Thompson, Hattie Dodson, Edna Brown, April 2006

Chapter Seventeen
1951-1955

Papa once said, "The Lord promised the bird a tree and the animals on the ground a hole in the log, but promised no man a home. That he would have to work for it from the sweat of his brow."

After several months of living in Ethel's house, it was time for us to leave and move on. I met a man, and he had a two-bedroom trailer. He said he would take twenty dollars a month for it because that's what the lot cost him to put it on. Me and the kids moved in, and we were real happy 'cause we had a house of our own. Of course, Ethel and them was just as good to us as they could be. She was like a sister. Whatever she had she would share with me, and whatever I had I would share with her. I started going with William Riddle six months after Shorty passed away. He'd tell the children, "Don't cry. Your daddy has gone to heaven, and he'll be watching after you." He was very comforting. He would hold me in his arms and he would say, "I'm here for you and the children, and we're going to make it." From the first day I met him he was always showing interest in me and the children. He always called Sue his little girl. He'd take her on his lap and love her up and tell her, "You're Daddy's little girl."

"My daddy's gone," Sue would tell him.

Then William would say, "I'm your daddy now."

William said to me one day, "Nellie, I'm going down to the cotton camps to work, and if you and the kids want to go with me to get out of town we'll all pile into my car and we'll take a few blankets and things that we need and go."

So I said, alright, I would like to do that. I hadn't been out to Salida for a while.

It was about thirty-five or forty miles, maybe a little further from where we was at to the cotton patch. It was during the time of Thanksgiving. There was acres and acres of cotton, and it brought back memories of Shorty and us meeting in West Texas. I remembered his kindness and his beautiful hair and his smile was always warm and welcome.

The kids was all big enough to where they would get right in, just like I would, and work and make every dime we could while we was there. William was sleepin' in his car. I sure wasn't havin' him in my bedroom with my children in one cabin. So, he was sleepin' in the car, and on a Sunday night it startin' pourin' down rain. It rained all night. He came over to the cabin the next mornin', and I fixed him a good hot cup of coffee and a hot biscuit and gravy.

We sat down to eat breakfast, and he reached over and put his hand on mine and said, "Nellie, I know this isn't the type of place or the way I planned on proposing to you, but will you marry me?" His question shocked me through. I had no intentions of marrying him because I had done failed twice, in a sense of the word, and my heart was still broken over Shorty. I didn't know what to say.

"You'll have to give me some time to think about it."

William taken baby Sue in his arms and hugged and kissed her and told her, "You tell your mama to say yes."

I just all but broke down in tears to think that somebody would want me and my children. I set there for a few minutes, and baby Sue said, "Mama, I want my daddy to be William Riddle."

"Yes, yes, of course," I told her.

William reached over and hugged and kissed me.

A man in the cotton fields sold him two gold band rings for twenty dollars, and the following day, after I told him I would marry him, it was still raining and William says, "I can't think of a better day to get married than today. What about you?"

"It's fine with me," I told him.

We left the children with Louise, and me and him headed for Fresno and were married by the justice of peace at the county courthouse.

William stayed down at the cotton fields so he could work during the rest of the holidays, while I come to Modesto to find a place to live and to put the children back in school. We pulled into a camp ground in Modesto and camped under an old shade tree across the street from the church. We all slept in the car that night, and the next mornin' whenever we woke up it was cold and damp and raining.

A man that owned the lot come up and said, "So, you've all decided to move in here!"

"No, sir, we haven't decided to move in here. We just had to have a place to park to sleep for the night."

"Let me sell you this lot."

I got out of the car and walked around on the lot. There was a chicken shed on the lot that hadn't been used in about three years. I turned and told Louise, "We could turn this henhouse into something livable and use the land to build a house on."

I was six months pregnant with my baby boy, David, at the time when we started fixing our henhouse. The shed was long and wide and would support about a thousand chickens at a time. We dug out all the dirt and leveled it so it would be smooth and hauled in soft carpet and rolled layer after layer over the dirt floors to trap heat in during the winter. Me and Louise went and bought rolls of tar paper and put it on the outside to keep the rain and wind out. I cut windows out and put clear, heavy plastic over to let in the sunlight. We sprayed the whole henhouse down with Lysol spray to get rid of any bugs and to keep it nice and clean. We hauled the extra dirt from the floor to the backyard to make a spring garden and tore about half of the henhouse down and made fencing out of the extra wood for the garden. We had an old canary-yellow table with matching chairs that was give to us, and it was the ugliest thing I ever seen, but it made a good eating table. I had my baby, David, while I lived in the henhouse.

I registered the kids in Modesto School District, and I went to work at CVC's, a dehydrator factory where they dried carrots, tomatoes, sweet bell peppers, and other vegetables. When I started to work there, why I was getting a dollar thirty-five an hour, and I thought I was making millions. I could put food on the table and pay off the land, and I bought new material to make the children clothes out of.

I always stacked up extra food like my mother and father had taught me to do. The neighbors would laugh about it and ask me why in the world I was buying all of those canned goods and keeping it. Then they would say, "Don't you know that little store is just right down there?"

I told them, "I know it is. But, I will tell you what—if you ain't got no money, then you can't go to the store."

Louise graduated from high school, and I made her the most beautiful dress you ever saw. It was long and pink and had full sleeves—I called them bellbottom sleeves, and a bow of ribbon that tied around the back. I took her to the beauty shop to get her fingernails polished for the first time in her life and her hair curled in ringlets. She looked just like a princess.

The graduation was outside of Modesto College. We set up on some hard wooden benches, and clustered together to watch Louise graduate. The principal stepped forward and hugged Louise when she graduated, and he handed her papers to her personally. He was showing appreciation of her graduating. He was aware of her coming to school and was so far behind and then she passed all the tests and pulled herself out of it.

They all threw their caps up, and Ruth run down off of the bench and grabbed Louise's cap and brought it back to me. It was a blessed day and a proud moment and something that I had looked forward to. I thought, *My first baby graduated. She made it!*

It was beautiful watching Louise smile, knowing that she had graduated. When she come back to where I was, she hugged all the children and said, "I'm gonna help Mama see that everyone of y'uns graduate."

I was forever grateful that my first baby had graduated from high school in Modesto. It brought back memories of the short time that I had gone to school in Richmond, Arkansas. I thought of Mrs. McGraw and how hard she tried to teach me, and it give me a pleasant thought and a rest of assurance that I had done what I had promised to do.

Almost a year later, I started building my house on the land I bought. I built a two-bedroom house with windows and doors and a hardwood floor. There was two men, Mr. Sugar and Mr. Banks, both of them were veterans, and they offered me their help. Mr. Banks only had one leg, and Mr. Sugar had but one arm, but they were a great help. Of course, there were things they couldn't do, but there were lots of things they could do to help me build my house for me and the children. I was very happy whenevern' we got the permit to move into the big house. I was overly excited about it. William had come home, and he said, "And you did this all by yourself?"

I said, "No sir, the veterans helped me."

After I had David, I would work nights at the hospital and a swing shift at CVC's. I hired a babysitter next door to help with the children. I had another baby in 1954, and her name was Leona May. She had coal black hair, big blue eyes, and only weighed three-and-a-half pound when she was born.

William come home from the cotton camps and was strung out on drugs. He was losing all the flesh off his bones. He looked awful. I didn't know what was wrong with him. We had a family of what I call dopers in Salida—people that just take anything—any kind of drugs and drinkin'. William got into drinkin' and drugs so bad until he got to where he was real ornery with me and the kids. He quit working completely and said he didn't see no reason he needed to work. He said these other men are gettin' by and they're not workin'. But, their wives and families was working.

I never knowed nothin' about drugs or wine or nothin' like that 'cause we all lived a pretty clean life—we all lived a Christian life. We went to church every time we had a chance, maybe every Sunday. Things went along just like that.

William would not work. He absolutely quit workin', and he got so strung out he would take every penny me and the kids would make that was extra that we didn't have to have for groceries. He couldn't speak a word unless he was cussin', and if he wasn't cussing me he was cussin' something else. He just cussed, cussed, and it was ugly, ugly. He kept gettin' worse and was losing all the flesh off his bones—that old dope was drying him up on the bone. He kept on, and he was so bad, and I stood it about as long as I could.

One particular night, I was workin' the night shift at CVC's. Thelma Morris, my next-door neighbor that I was ridin' with, worked with me until about two-thirty that morning. Whenevern' we got home, William wouldn't let me in the house. He was all messed up on them drugs and the wine. It was cold and wet, and I was freezin' to death. I had no place to get in out of the weather, and he wouldn't let me in.

I could hear the kids screamin' and cryin' and so I went to the window and called out to them. I told them not to cry and that we would take care of this situation in the mornin'. I stood in the shoulder of the house, soaking wet and shivering from the wind and cold rain. I was so tired I could hardly stand up. I had worked hard at my job to support me and the family, and here he was all messed up on drugs and keeping me locked out of my own house that I had built. I wondered if I would live through this. I prayed all the time I was out there, *Lord, give me strength to make it through the night.*

I thought, *I'm not gonna put up with this. I won't tolerate him being all wiped out on drugs and not letting me into my own house. I'm gonna take care of this situation and never get into a situation like this again.* I had learned my lesson from him. It didn't matter what he'd done or said later, it would never change that situation.

It was comin' daylight, and Louise came to the window and called out to me, "Mama, he's fell asleep." She let me in the house, and I changed my wet clothes and shoes and walked across the street to the neighbors and asked her for a ride to my attorney's office.

I went into my attorney, and I was shakin' from being out in that rain all night. I told him what happened. "William is so strung out on drugs and wine until he is makin' me and the children miserable."

He said, "Why don't you just sign these papers and get you a divorce?"

"This is exactly what I want—a divorce from William Riddle. I want to divorce him for once and for all. I can't get him to stop doin' the drugs, and he is so mean and hateful, and he hasn't done a day's work now in heaven knows when."

I divorced William Riddle right then and there.

Chapter Eighteen
1957

The drugs have been awful. They have destroyed family after family, not just the poor people but the middle class people and the rich. Not just the ones that are sick and dead from them, but the mothers and the fathers and the sisters and the brothers and everything that's in its region.

It started here in about 1957. Drugs covered the whole scene of Modesto. There for a while it got terrible. I didn't get past it, either. I had some children, my own precious children, that have been taught from birth not to even take an aspirin. But, Lord, they did it. Louise got into drugs in the worst way. I was hurt to think that my own child would get into them. I didn't know which way to turn. Every time someone would show up at my place with their drugs, I would run them off. I was even offered the drugs a dozen times or more, but I had courage and guts enough to say, "No, thank you. Now get that out of here and don't come back to my place no more."

At one time I had some people in here from out of state, and they had come by to see me. The bad part of it was they thought it was such a nice quiet place, but by the time they got all settled into my house, we heard ten gunshots. When they got through shooting, there were eight down—all around the houses and the river—all shot down. Of course, at that time they hadn't shot any of my folks. There was enough to drive a sane person insane.

The very next night there was another shootout across the street in front of my house. One guy got shot in the foot and in the chest. They kept on doing this. I had been seeing signs of drugs all over the place.

The addicts used to take anything they could. They would take the bread right off my table if they thought they would get a fix off of it. It was disgraceful. If you had a hose, they would take it. I had my house broken in to during the earlier part of the drug scene three different times, and the policemen was raiding everybody's houses. They finally discovered that I wasn't doing this kind of stuff. I was trying to keep others from doing it.

As years went by in the early 60s, it kept getting worse and worse. My next daughter, Ruth, got into it. Half of whole families were into it and they would lose three or four kids, sometimes all at the same time. At one time, there were twenty-eight deaths in our county from overdosing on drugs in less than a week. The sheriff's department was doing everything they could to put a stop to it. They'd wave as they'd go by because they knew what kind of person I was. They knew I wasn't going to put up with none of it, and that I would try to straighten up those that are into it.

I had been keeping the kids in close because there had been so many drive-by shootings. One day I had several little grandkids here at the house, and I heard a racket. I looked out the window and could see the edge of one man, and so I put all the kids in the hallway. I had a pile of blankets and pillows there so they could lie down when any shooting started.

About that time I looked out the window and saw a man draggin' a blond-headed man inside my gate. I told the kids, "Stay down and don't get up."

My granddaughter began to cry. "Grandma, they'll kill you!"

I told her, "We're inside, and we won't get hurt."

I walked to the window and shouted to them, "I'm the only grown up here—there is only little children here. If you have any sense at all you will get out of here because the FBI and sheriff's department will be here soon."

The man took a look at me and nodded at his friend and then began to load up his gun. I figured it would be better for me to go out and talk to them before they started shooting.

They all got out of my yard and before they got to the corner, I think the sheriff got part of them. It was a terrible scene right then. It was one terrifying thing after another around here for two or three years. It was really bad.

One time I was sitting on my front porch, and I heard a gunshot. I had a big bunch of birds in a cage sitting in the front yard where I could feed them and watch them. I thought they were real pretty parakeets. Then, I saw one of the birds fall off the roost. The children were coming around the corner of the house, and I hollered to them to get way down and crawl into the house and get into the hallway because they could get shot. Somebody else heard the shots and called the sheriff and it wasn't but just minutes before the sheriff had come. They asked me where I thought the bullets was coming from, and I told them I didn't know. The sheriff gathered a bunch of people up and took them off to jail. This was only one of the bad scenes we had out here.

It was awful. You never knew when you laid down if your children were going to be safe when they woke up.

Chapter Nineteen

In 1963, I moved from the house where I was livin' to another house, on account of the drug scene. I found out the drugs were as bad here as they was in the other house. They were all over the whole state of California.

I was still working at CVC's, and I opened up a drapery shop. I felt real secure in the drapery business because I knowed what I was doin'. I had hired four women to help me do the sewin', and two men.

One of the women that was workin' for me had a nephew that was in the service, and that was Mr. Thompson—Dallas H. Thompson. She was talkin' to me about him, and she said, "He's such a likable person, and I would like for you to meet him."

I had spent twelve years by myself and intended to spend the rest of my life by myself. I wasn't interested in no man 'cause I had failed three different times with lifetime partners. I had felt like I had had enough. I didn't want to put up with another man as long as I lived, and, in fact, I had pretty much shut the world off when it come to men folks. I was scared to even speak to one hardly.

A few days later, when Dallas walked through the door, here was this big, handsome guy all dressed up in his uniform and come waltzin' in there like King Fruit. He says, "So, you're Nellie?"

I said, "Yes, I'm her."

"I need some seat covers made."

"Well, what do you want them made of?"

He walked over there to a big roll of red velvet, I mean a beautiful red velvet, and says, "What does this sell a yard?"

I said, "Well, what do you want if for?"

He said, "Well, I'll tell ya. I've got a car out here and I had some kids playin' in the backseat, and they spilt stuff all over it, and it's my new car and it looks all ugly. I'd like to get a new set of seat covers for the whole thing."

I said, "Alright, that's fine," and I got my tape measure and my book that I wrote everything down on—the measurements and the sizes and everything—and we started out the door. He got too close to me from following me, and I turned around and said, "You show me where the car is."

He went out and unlocked the car, it was a four-door car, and opened the doors. I said, "Now, you go over there, and I'll get over here, and we'll take the measurements. It takes two of us to take car seat measurements, you know. One person can do it, but it's uncertain if you're gonna get a good fit." I said, "You just hold that end of the tape."

We both leaned in over the backseat to get the measurements, and would you know, that man hauled off and kissed me! I slapped the water right outta him. I slapped him until his face was as red as a turkey gobbler's mouth.

"Don't you ever, ever think you can take advantage of me like that and get by with it!"

Of course, I was a pretty strong woman back then. I was only about forty-five years old and I could pick up a hundred-and-fifty pound roll of fabric and carry it across the room, or carry it anywhere it needed to be carried. I lifted fabric around all day.

So, lo and behold, he accepted my rebuke and apologized to me. I'll swear, when I started to measure the front seats, he done the same thing again, and yes, I did. I slapped him even harder than I did the first time. "I don't know if I even want your job if you can't be man enough to keep your hands off me and quit kissin' me. I don't even need your business."

It was real funny. He apologized again. He said, "I don't know why I did that!"

I said, "Well, you better know, and you'd better not do it no more."

He said, "I promise. Please make me the red velvet seat covers. I've got money in my pocket to pay you for them. In fact, I'm gonna pay you up front."

About that time Leona come in, and she was crying. David had taken her bicycle and taken a wheel off of it and she couldn't ride it. Dallas petted my baby up and told her, "Don't worry about it, honey, I'll just show him something. I'll just buy you a new bicycle."

But, when he went and got the bicycle, he got two of them—one for her, and one for him.

That started him. From then on, I couldn't even throw my water out the door without hittin' him in the face with it. We went along for two months, and one day he come over and I was just getting dressed and come out and he grabbed me and hugged and kissed me. Before I could get my hand up, he grabbed my hand, and he said, "Don't you do it! Don't you do it!"

I said, "Okay."

He said, "Would you marry me?"

I said, "No! I can't marry you. I don't want to marry you. I don't want to get married. I don't want no man in my life."

"Well, can I hang around a little while longer?"

"I guess so. I guess you can hang around a little while longer."

Time come and went, and he had to go back to the service. Before he got ready to go overseas, he asked me, "Please, please marry me. I'm gonna give you somethin' you'll be real proud of."

I said, "If you think it's gonna be another kid, I wouldn't be proud of that, 'cause I done had six babies, and that's all I could handle."

He said, "Oh, no, no. I wished you'd just come and go with me tomorrow. I'm gonna take care of a little business over here. If you just come and go with me."

I said, "I can't take off a day of work and go with you. I've got a job to do and a livin' to make."

So, he went on, and he told me, "I'm gonna re-enlist. I can help you with the children and all while I'm in the service."

I said, "Well, alright. If that's the way you feel about it."

He asked me again to marry him. He asked me about fourteen times to marry him, and I finally told him, "If you ask to marry me again, I will quit you, and I will never speak to you again."

He was very careful about asking me again.

The day he got ready to go back overseas to Guam, he hugged and kissed me and said, "Please don't hit me. I've got to tell you something. I want you to be my wife. I'm not asking you to marry me, I'm just asking you to be my wife. You're the hardest woman I've ever seen in my life to get to say yes."

Well, he went to Guam and was gone for a long time. I felt relieved whenevern' he left, but every time I turned around, my mind would center on him and what was happening over in Guam. He wrote me about once a month and always sent a little money for the kids. I thought he might be the very person to be good to me and the children. He was kind and he was always buying my children something, and no man had ever done that before.

He served thirty-one years in the service, and in the last couple months he was over there they had discovered he had picked up the Agent Orange. They brought him home on an ambulance airplane to Merced. His sister come and took me down there to see him. He broke down and started crying because he thought he'd never live to see me again. It broke my heart, too, to think that somebody would care enough about me and the children to go and serve the rest of his time for our country and come home to me. They kept him in the hospital until they got him past the first issue of the Agent Orange. While he was there I helped him everyway I could.

After Dallas got back from Guam, he was hesitant to ask me to marry him, but, one day he said, "This can't go on this way. You can't manage with the children all by yourself when I'm willing to help you."

I told him, "I will not give up my children for no man under the sun. I won't give up my family for nobody."

He said, "Honey, I'm not asking you to give up your family. I'm asking you to give them to me. I don't have a family. I don't have a livin' soul to leave nothin' to. If I was to die tomorrow, I wouldn't be able to leave nobody nothin'."

I broke down and cried to think that he'd served his country a lifetime and had nobody, and I was the person he really wanted. I felt like he was my bright and shining armor that had come to take care of me and my children. I felt a security with him, and I felt safe. I knowed there wouldn't be anybody coming in, running over me or the children, 'cause he would take care of it. I had seen that much good in him. I felt like he was Lord sent and that I was being stubborn not to accept it.

I finally got married to him in October 1965, and my life begin to change. It was much easier now. The older children were all grown, and me and him spent a lot of time together. He made every minute count. Every time we would get together, he would always make it something special. He was a true soldier. A true veteran.

I had many happy times with him. We went places together and enjoyed each other's love. We went dancing and to moving shows. We did everything together. I was more than grateful for him. He proved hisself, and his love many times over. He had a way of taking his hand and rubbing it across the back of my neck and relaxing me, and nine times out of ten it led me to loving him and understanding him. I'd usually turn around and put my arms around him and love and kiss him.

Some days I'd work nine or ten hours. He would come in and catch me and hold me up close to him, then rub his hand across my neck and say, "Let's take off and go have supper. Or let's take off and go for a little drive."

One day Dallas said to me, "Now get all prettied up, Nellie." He just got finished putting in thirty-one years in the service, and it was his birthday. His friends were giving him a birthday party down at Castle Air Force base. I put on a tight bra, a low-cut red dress, and a string of gold beads around my neck. Those beads hung in the opening of my breasts, and I had a pair of black heels on that really showed off my legs and my feet.

When we walked onto the dance floor he had his hand on my shoulder, kinda around my neck, and we were laughing and talking. I told him, "Happy birthday, dear," and he said, "Thank you, honey, you look like a million."

I guess there was a hundred-and-fifty guys there, and only about eight or ten women. He let me dance with four different men that was there, and then he decided he wanted to dance with me, and that's whenever the confusion started. When we were dancing, just at the finish of the music, a young sergeant come up and tapped me on the shoulder and said, "The next set is mine."

Dallas says, "Like hell it is, Sarge, this is my wife."

I just smiled about it. I didn't dare laugh out loud 'cause it would have been a fight on hand. Then Dallas says to me, "We better go."

He could not stand for another man to get too close. Even though he got fired up about things every now and again, Dallas loved me and helped with the education of my children.

All of my children graduated from high school—Louise, Ruth, George, Sue, Leona, and David. Me and Dallas went to the children's graduations together, and he was real supportive with it. He was real happy for each one of them.

Well, it was very simple and very understandable. In 1965 when I married Dallas I was forty-seven years-old, and thought I knowed right from wrong and what love was and what it was intended for. But, I know when I finally found Dallas, I felt free to love him, and love him again. This relieved a lot of pain and suffering in my heart that I had hung on to for years. He made me feel secure. I felt it didn't matter what happened, I knew he would take care of me.

Love and compassion of another person is something that is seldom ever seen or heard of. True love is hard to find. It's hard to discover. It's something so many people never find. But I found it, and carried it to the end.

Chapter Twenty
1980

I was at a laundromat in Modesto one evening when my daughter Ruth appeared to me in a vision. She was lying in a box. I thought, *Oh, dear Lord. Something's happened to Ruth!* I quickly gathered my washing 'cause I knew there was something wrong with my baby. Of course, she was thirty-two years old, but she was still my baby.

She and her husband had left me about two months prior and moved to Washington state. They had gotten into the drugs and were leaving Modesto to try and get out of the drug scene. Leona, too, had married a drug addict and began using them, and eventually my baby boy, David, caught on. It was a nightmare, each person passing drugs on to the next.

I hadn't heard from Ruth since she'd moved; not until I was at the laundromat that night. On my way to my car, a good friend to Ruth came up to me in the parking lot and said, "Do you know they're burying your daughter today?"

I said, "No, sir," and then I started to cry. He told me he'd heard they were burying her in Big Bear, Washington, and he didn't know what had happened.

I quickly drove off and came home and told my husband, Dallas, "There is something wrong goin' on with Ruth. I saw a friend on my way home from the wash house, and I don't think he was playing a prank on me because I saw something."

"What did you see?"

"I saw Ruth in a casket when I was down at the wash house. I'm gonna go find her in Washington."

"You can't go without me."

Dallas was a sick man at the time. Sick with emphysema and asthma, but he told me, "You can't go on your own because you will get crying and feeling depressed, and no telling what would happen."

We got our station wagon ready. Dallas made a bed in the back end, and I threw in some clothes, and we headed out for Washington. We drove and drove and drove. I thought we would never get there. It seemed like the longest miles I had ever seen in my life, and, the longer I went the sicker Dallas got.

We finally made it to Big Bear, and I went to a little church house where the funeral was held. I talked with the minister there and he told me they had buried Ruth yesterday at about two o'clock in the afternoon—that she'd died of a hemorrhage of the brain. He told me where Ruth's children were, and I wrote it down.

I was tired and worn out and my husband was sick, but I never stopped. I put the foot to the metal and drove as fast as I could to get there. It seemed like I had to get there, and nothin' was gonna stand in my way.

My daughter had three children: Kathy, Margaret Ruth, and Linda Roberta. This lady they were staying with at the time was trying to adopt them out from under me. "I'm a takin' the kids," she said. "I need them for the income." She told me they were going to court at one o'clock that afternoon and then she would have the kids.

The kids came in, and I told them to get what they wanted out of the house and to get into my car. I run and jumped in the car and the kids had done climbed in the car 'cause I had practically raised them. They had been around me all their lives and they knowed that I was their grandma and they knowed that I had come after them.

When I got to the court, here was the kid's daddy and this other lady that wanted to adopt them. The dad was in no condition to take the kids, and the judge stood up and said, "Listen. This is these children's legal grandmother and she drove all the way from California with a sick husband and she's gonna take these babies out of here. We don't need all this in court, we just need the grandma."

He asked the two oldest to stand up and tell him who they wanted to go with. "Do you want to go with your daddy or do you want to go with your grandma?" One didn't speak any faster than the other did. They both said, "We want to go with our Grandma. We're ready!" The judge give me the children

This woman came out of there just a-cussin' every breath she was taking. She didn't know why the judge gave me the kids. It's because the judge was a smart man and he knew they would be safe with me. Their daddy came out, and he said, "Well, since you've got the kids, can I have visiting rights?"

I said, "Of course you can. I will never keep these children from anybody, but I'll raise them and I'll take care of them."

We got in the car and we started out back to California. As we were coming into Olympia it looked like it had begun to snow. I thought, *Oh, Lord, it's gonna start snowing on us.* Dallas was in the back of the car, and it sounded like he was dying. I couldn't hardly breathe myself, but I kept pushing.

The snow got on the windshield, and I rolled down the window and reached over and swiped the windshield a couple of times with an old shirt and discovered it wasn't snow. It was ashes.

I drove for several hours without stopping, just long enough to get a drink of water. We came up through Eugene and stopped at a filling station and the guy at the station said, "Have you all heard the news?"

I said, "No sir, we've been traveling."

He said, "Mount Saint Helen has erupted. The bigger part of it is over with."

We didn't hear anything else about it until a little later, and then we heard about it on the news. I started driving like crazy 'cause I had to get my husband to the hospital. We noticed the ashes started to fall less and less the further away we got from Eugene.

When I finally got into Modesto, Dallas was gasping for breath. The ashes from the volcano caused his asthma and emphysema to be worse. I opened the door to our trailer and put the kids in and rushed him straight to the hospital. I held his driver's license and his medical card up to the guard that was letting me through, and he waved me right on in and carried me to the emergency area.

After a few minutes they lost him. They knocked him around a bit, and he came around, and finally got him to take a breath. The doctor give him a couple of shots and then put him on the breathing machine for a while.

I didn't lose my husband at this time, and thank God.

We started raisin' Ruth's three children. Kathy was about fifteen years old, Margaret Ruth was eleven, and Roberta was eight. I put them in school, and all three later graduated from high school. In my life, school was one of the most important things there is. Everybody has got to go to school because the more you learn, the more you earn. That's my teaching.

Chapter Twenty-One
1981

In 1981 I was taken down with heart troubles. I went to the hospital, and the doctor wanted to put in a heart valve, an output valve, and take out my right kidney. He had it all drawed-up on paper. He said I couldn't possibly live over six months with all the ailments, if that long. One doctor got brave enough to tell me to close my business down. I was still doing custom drapes at the time.

They sent me to another clinic to be examined, and they said I desperately had to have the operations—all three of them. They would do it all at one time so I wouldn't be in so much pain. But they didn't know me. I didn't intend to have 'nare one of them operations, and I haven't had nary an operation yet—'nare a broken a bone. Even with all I been through.

They let me out of the clinic and coming home I thought, *Well, if I could just end this thing it would be a miracle.* I never did believe in people taking their own lives, but in this chance I figured it would be worth it. All the suffering that I would have to go through, and they give me only a ten percent chance out of a hundred of getting off the operation table alive.

When I got to the Seventh Street Bridge in Modesto I thought, I'll just park my car here, and I'll jump off into the river and it will be all over with. When I got up to the rail to look down, the water looked like it was only about two or three foot deep. I could see the bottom all over. I thought, I'll jump off in there and break both legs, and then I'll have that to put up with, plus what else I'm putting up with. I know the Spirit was telling me not to do this. I went back and got into the car and broke down and cried like a baby. I told the Lord, "If you need me, you're gonna to have to take care of me. I don't know what to do. I'm at my rope's end." I left it all up to the Lord. Between me and Him we sure had a battle with it.

We finally moved into the new house where I'm living now. Dallas was real sick, and was in and out of Livermore Veteran's with the effects of Agent Orange, and we had this house full of children—twelve of them all together. I was taking care of all of them, trying to make a living, and trying to do the best I could.

I couldn't see no way of me taking that operation. I had been to the doctor, and I had all these pills they give me to take. I had a big, black purse, like most women and men do now, where I kept them. I was to take twenty-four tablets a day, and I don't like medicine no how. It was killing me!

That fall was coming by then, and I was up to the end of the six months the doctors had give me to live. They wanted to operate on me, put me on a pacemaker, and take one of my kidneys out. Well, I couldn't stand the thought of being butchered up that way. They kept telling me, "You can't make it." So I quit going to see them. I began to pray, "Lord, if you want me here and you want me to do this job, you're going to have to take care of me." I couldn't see any other way out, only to hold onto the Lord. That's all I was doing was holding onto Him and letting Him take it away. I held onto Him tighter than I'd ever held on in my life.

The great spirits began to show me things.

I went and done bought me a bed to die in, and I had it in the living room. I didn't want to be in the bed with my husband and him gettin' up with the shock of me being dead. I was having a spell with my heart, and it was so bad my arms went numb, and my feet and legs went numb, too. I kept getting worse and worse, and I got down to where I weighed one-hundred-and-eighteen pounds. I was on my bed and the Spirit—He's such a beautiful thing—come quite often for the next month or more. He showed me I needed to go in to the mountains.

Time went by and the spirits kept showing me things. There was this little old man about five-foot tall, with little slanted eyes, and grey hair down his back in a braid. I couldn't tell if he was Indian or Chinese, but it didn't make much difference 'cause he was bringing me a message. He would get right on top of this mountain of white minerals and look out over the valley where all the herbs were.

In the next session of the spirit appearing to me, the little man with the white hair appeared again on top of the mineral healing mountain, and here was this grey light from heaven. It was so bright you could have picked a pin off the ground. It was reaching wide out from the heavens, right down where I was and right down where the man was that was gonna hand out the water. There was abreast of people as far as my eyes could see. Sick people and crippled people, and they all wanted a drink of this healing water that was coming off the minerals on the side of the mountain.

The little man took a drink and started handing out the cups of water. I seen that this man needed help so I got a cup, and I begin to hand out the healing water. But first of all, I taken the cup that they handed me and I drank 'cause I wanted the people to know that it was gonna heal them. As we began to get everybody a cup of the healing water, they would drink the water and then they would go down the hill and roll in the pool of minerals.

As they were leaving the pond of white minerals, they left their wheelchairs and walkers and canes behind. This went on for hours. Finally, we got to the end of this great long line of people—big, little, old and young, black, white, brown, or yellah—whatever color the skin was, it didn't make a bit of difference. They all drank the healing water and rolled in the minerals.

Whenevern' it come time for me and the little man, we marched ourselves down and followed the rest of them and got right down there into the minerals, head and all—clothes and everything. Our bodies were completely covered.

And the last of the vision was me and the little man on top of the mountain. He pulled up some bushes with long roots hanging from them. He held them out from his body in his right hand. He dipped them into the water, and the water dripping off this herb was red. It looked like blood. He turned to me and said, "This is as far as I'm going with you. I'm going back to where I came from," and the spirits lifted him from there beside me and the spiritual prayer was over.

The great blessings had come. I had seen that vision, and it was beautiful! You can't imagine seeing hundreds of people being healed, and all their wheelchairs and canes and everything left behind.

The visions I had showed me my health was in God's hands and that I had to rely on the goodness of the earth to get well. I remembered the old Indian medicine man that used the minerals and the herbs to pull the polio out of my body, and I got past it. I was able to walk and work and help others. I was well-blessed through the herbs and the minerals.

I remembered my mother taking the dogwood limbs and brushing our feet and backs to keep the tics and fleas off of us. I remembered my grandfather, the Indian medicine man, who was forever healing and working with somebody that was sick. He had an understanding of God and of the earth and the herbs that would heal the body.

As time went on I started feeling a little better, and the following spring I went to the mountains. I wanted to follow the deer and the bear and find out what herbs and minerals the animals were eating. I wanted to improve my knowledge of the herbs that are good for man. My grandfather told me when I was little, "If we follow the deer and the bear and see what they eat, we find much knowledge and we find what's healing. There are many things that man copies after the knowledge of the bear."

I took some of my grandchildren into the mountains, and it was beautiful. Everybody wanted to pan for gold so they could make enough for their school clothes the following year. Everybody but me. I wasn't interested in the gold. I was more interested in knowin' what the bear was eatin'.

I started exploring the mountains and saw a bear. It was a big brown bear that stood about as tall as me when it straightened up. I watched her as she began to eat a tiny, white berry. She dug down and got some roots, and the babies dug where she was diggin'. They all began to chew around on the roots and began to eat on them.

I followed her quite a ways across the mountain, and she led me to a big blackberry patch. Wild blackberries was comin' in at that time. She ate off of the berry bush and several other different herbs, which led me to believe they were okay for man to eat. I followed her back up to Beaver Creek, and then she went across the creek, so I left her there and come back to the campsite.

The next evening I began to watch for the deer. The deer began to gather. There was about eight of them—big old buck deer. It was a beautiful sight. They were a tan color and had white cottontails, and the ears and noses were darker than the rest of the body, which made them stand out.

I heard a sound like drums. A real soft and mellow sound. I sat on a tree stump and watched to see what the deer were gonna do and I listened to the drums. It was the most beautiful sound! Different nationalities were playing, everyone in beat. It was soothing. It was something you can't ever imagine hearing or seeing—deer sittin' with their noses up and ears back, not making a sound or a move. And, as many birds as there are in the mountains—not even a bird made a sound. All during the time of this music.

I've been back to the mountains many seasons to listen to the beating of the drums. The drums in the mountains sing. They sing some of the most beautiful songs you ever heard. Of course, I always call that mile through there the sacred mile—where you can hear the drums. Where the deer all get up on the mountainside and raise their heads and look straight into the heavens and not even a squirrel will make a sound. Not even a bird. And the deer look straight into the heavens until the last two of the drums is played.

Everything in hearing distance is as still as a mouse. Nothin' moves, not even a rustle of a leaf until that music is over. It's the most tender-lovin' music you've ever heard in your life, and it's all done with drums. It all comes from the tenderness and the love of the drums. I often dream of goin' back there and listenin' to those drums—the soothing of the heart and the happiness of the wilderness. It's deep in the beautiful mountains.

And this had been a little better than thirty years ago. I was sixty-five years old then, and I'm ninety years old now. I'm ever so thankful to be here. I'm thankful for God that he give me the strength and energy and told me and showed me what to do. God can do that. If you're a believer of God, the faith within God can heal most anything, straighten out most anything, and put you on the right track. God will help us if we ask Him. I am grateful to my spirits. Jesus is the greatest spirit of all spirits—to my knowledge.

I'm an Indian medicine lady just like my grandfather John T. Williams was an Indian medicine man. He'd go out and dig the herbs from the mountains and the creek beds, and he'd cook it and bottle it up and give it to sick people. My mother used to help my grandfather put the herbs and minerals in bottles so they could be sold to the Indians and other people.

I do the Indian herbs and the minerals for people that are sick and people that have all kind of illnesses. When I got down sick, I related back to my childhood and my grandfather treating the people for illnesses that other doctors don't know about today, and I went to doctoring myself. I was give only six months to live if I didn't have the operations, but I went to taken the herbs and the medicine, got well, and went back to work.

I thank God that He give me the knowledge to turn back to my grandfather—the Indian medicine man. God give us the understanding of the herbs to heal everything and everybody.

In the next few months, I begin collecting the herbs and the minerals that grew in the mountains and taking them to heal my own body, just as I had seen my granddad do and just as I had seen in my visions. I begin to drink spring water from out of the mountains, and I grew strong and healthy. Since then, I've helped many people with the minerals and the herbs to overcome illness. By some people of the world I'm known by Lady Nellie, the Indian medicine woman.

Chapter Notes:

In the words of Nellie: "Around the time I began using the herbs and minerals for healing, I was given the beautiful Andoran's. They are beautiful stones that have a glass-like appearance and come in many colors and many shapes. They are as original as people themselves. Some people use them for healing and others enjoy the beauty of them, in the sunshine or on a windowsill. I love the beauty of them and the gathering of them from one friend to another. When I first discovered them, I begin giving them away and was grateful that people passed them from one person to another. They've brought many people together. I have two large brown stones, which is called Indian Pearl, right inside my gate. They keep down disturbance. When people see the brown stones they stop their bickering."

Chapter Twenty-Two
October 1984

One morning Dallas had a bad spell with his heart. I was in the living room, and I heard him struggling for breath, and I run into the bedroom. I throwed the covers off of him and got him on his feet and into the car. I carried him from the house over to Livermore Hospital. He had been in and out of the hospital for the past twelve years on account of him having asthma, Agent Orange, and emphysema.

I was raising Louise's and Ruth's children because somebody had to be responsible for their kids going to school, and that was me. I was taking care of Louise's one son, and Ruth's three daughters, and Dallas helped me.

Me and my daughter Sue were sitting there beside Dallas in the hospital room, and he was begging for some water. I asked the nurse if he could have some water and she said, "No, but you can mop his mouth out with a little sponge. He has too much fluid in around his heart."

About that time the lights went out in the whole hospital for forty-five minutes without any backup. I was by Dallas's bedside and a nurse had a candle and told us to follow her into the waiting room. There were shadows in the hallway, but my eyes were so full of tears I could hardly see them. I heard footsteps running in every direction but not many voices other than the people running from one bedroom to another, trying to save the veterans.

During this time the nurses took turns pumping air into Dallas's mouth and throat to keep him alive. They wouldn't let me in there; they wouldn't open the door for me. The nurses kept coming out telling me, "We're doing everything we can."

"We're losing him," I told them.

I got in a chair and sat in the waiting room, close to the door so I could get to him if they'd let me in there. I remembered all the pain and suffering he'd been through over the past twelve years with the Agent Orange.

After forty-five minutes, the lights finally came on and the air began to flow, so Dallas could breathe again. The nurses opened the door and let me go in and see him. I caught him by his hand, and he squeezed my hand and tried to open his eyes to see me. I said, "Honey, now you'll get all the air you need." I continued holding his hand and comforting him. I rubbed his forehead and began to rub his legs because his leg was cramping.

He had served his country well, and his body really showed the scars from over the years. He was eat up with that Agent Orange. It caused cancer all over his body and all in his face. In fact, five years before, an old service doctor said, "I don't want you to so much as kiss this man." They taken out all of his glands below his navel and went in and operated on him. He could not support sex. He just wasn't there. For five years there we couldn't even hug and kiss each other, but we were both there for each other.

I tried and tried, time and time again, to get him to take the herbs and the minerals, but he refused me. He said he had some good doctors and that they would take care of him. He didn't believe in the natural cures. He thought that they were for the Indians and not for the white folks. That's what he'd say.

I was scared to death that I was losing him. He had been my survivor for so long and had been so good to me until I knowed I was losing that part of me for good. He took away a lot of pain and misery that had built up inside me over the years. I remembered a song he used to sing to me called, "What could I do to melt your cold, cold heart and let me love again." I thought about how hard he tried to get me to marry him, and now to think I was losing him. He made every day a pleasure and built faith and confidence in me to where I could believe in someone again.

Dallas opened his eyes and took one look at me and then closed his eyes and he was gone. Right then and there, I had lost him. He was gone! It was a sad thing. Me and my daughter Sue was both there.

He was the only veteran that died during the lights going out in the Livermore Hospital, and it was a sad day. The Air Force give him a ten-gun salute over his grave when we put him away. They rolled up his flag and put it in my arms. It was a blessing in disguise, I guess you'd say, because he wouldn't be suffering anymore, but I sure would miss my sweetheart.

Friends and neighbors came and brought me a lot of good food. Some among them were veterans, but this wasn't good enough for me. I had to have a clear understanding of that hospital. I went to an attorney, and wouldn't you know it, that attorney was a veteran. He told me, "Nellie you have a legal court trial coming, but I want you to think about something. You know your husband suffered, and suffered death for twelve years. But he's gone now. Suing won't bring your husband back."

I had time to think this over. I had a prayer with God. I told God what the attorney had said—it wouldn't help anything because it wouldn't bring my husband back.

I sat there for about thirty minutes with the attorney and neither one of us said anything to the other. I finally asked him to forget the lawsuit. I told him I loved the veterans and have helped them all my life. I told him my grandfather and great-grandfather were veterans. He said, "Nellie, you've made it all these years. It would take three men to fill your place. You've made the right decision."

Since this day, I have helped thousands of veterans. I am an Indian herbalist, and I have helped and healed many veterans in my day. I've given them money, food, and a hope for God.

If one comes to me cold and hungry, I will feed him and clothe him, but I can't take away the hurt that he's had and accepted in life.

I remembered Great-uncle Chief Pushmataha, who brought peace to the whites and the Indians. He was my first veteran. Then I remembered my great-granddad, Chief Nitakechi, that signed the peace treaty with the white man. He was another great veteran, and I always honored him because he said, "I will give up my life to save my people." That's the same thing these veterans have done. They've given up their lives and livelihoods and their happiness to save this beautiful country.

I've gotten rewards on my wall where I've helped the veterans. I didn't do it because I wanted that reward; I did it because it needed to be done. And in many cases it had to be done. They put their right foot forward and saved America—Amen, brother. Amen, sister, and God Bless!

I've worked hard, but I haven't been through half as much as our poor veterans have that saved this country and our families. God bless 'em. Everyone of them helped saved America.

Dallas made one of the finest daddy's I believe I'd ever seen. He loved those kids and helped provide for them for twenty-one years. There was a long period of time things went wrong, but he stuck right in there and helped me with those kids. Whenevern' my daughter Ruth passed away, and I had her three children—he stuck right in there and helped. Until this very day I ain't got a kid that won't stand up and say, "Dallas H. Thompson was my Daddy!" He was one of the best, and every one of them, from the oldest to the youngest, loved him.

Today has been a hard one. To put this all on paper and to bring out all the things that happened during the time of his death. It's been real hard on me.

Now you know why and how I met Mr. Thompson. We met each other fightin' and ended up lovin' each other at the end.

Chapter Twenty-Three

My husband William Riddle finally left the county and went to Arizona. The sheriff department come and told me he had passed away and that I needed to come and help bury him. Drugs dragged him down until we went to his funeral. He looked like he was a hundred years old when he finally died. Drugs dried all the meat right off his bones and left just his skin.

The man at the funeral home told us there wasn't a minister in the little town. David said he would go fill the car up so we could make it to the cemetery. While he was out there fillin' the car up with gas, our minister from Modesto drove up and said, "David, what are you doing in Arizona?"

David called his minister by name and said, "I'm out here burying my daddy, and I don't have a minister."

He said, "Well, you do now!"

This minister loved David and Leona up and helped them put their daddy away in Phoenix, at Pine Cemetery. On the east side of the cemetery was Arthur G. Bixler and on the south side was William Riddle—two husbands buried in the same cemetery. How many times could this ever happen, I wonder.

There was only six people at his funeral. It was me, Leona and her husband, David and his wife, and the minister. William had no friends, nobody—just drugs until he killed hisself.

We tried to buy some flowers to put on the grave, but everything was so dry and hot and windy and there wasn't a flower in the town. Leona got a piece of dry cactus and laid it on the head of his grave. It wasn't green, it was dry, too.

We sang, and the only song I could remember was, "When the Roll Is Called up Yonder, I'll be there." I thought of Mama and all the flowers she had at her funeral, and here William was dead and didn't have a flower to put on his grave. His funeral brought back a lot of hard memories. My mother had just had a baby girl, Ruth Irline, and we had buried her, and then Mama was the second one that passed away. It left such an awful heartache because I didn't know how many more I was going to lose. It looked like we was gonna lose my daddy, too. Since I've lost my mother, I've lost so many others until I feel I'm stronger and can take it now, but it still hurts so bad.

Soon after William died, Louise overdosed on drugs. She had just gotten out of the hospital and got herself straightened out, and then she goes on another spree of drugs. One day she asked me how much money I had and I told her I had a twenty dollar bill and she said, "You give it here! Give it to me!"

I told her, "I don't even have any milk or a slice of bread. I can't give you the last dime I have. I'll give you half of what I have."

She said, "I won't have it that way," and she snatched it out of my hands and told me I could make my own bread. "I am a drug addict and an alcoholic, and I can't do without it. You've got the money, and I know you've got plenty of it," she'd say.

I finally gave in rather than fight with her over it.

The next morning, Louise's next door neighbor called and told me that Louise was down on the floor and that she couldn't get her up. She asked me what she should do. I told her to call an ambulance and call the sheriff's department and they would probably be there by the time I got there. I drove as fast as I could, and I got there and the sheriff's department and the ambulance had just got there. They went in to get her up, and she was laying there naked in the middle of the floor, and they covered her with blankets. The sheriff's department said, "Nellie, who is this?"

I said, "This is my oldest daughter, Louise."

He almost broke in tears because he had just lost his son in a shoot-out at the park a few weeks before this.

"My goodness, I didn't know you had anybody this age."

"Yes, sir, she's my daughter."

And then Louise said, "I'm not her daughter! I don't know who this old bag is that's trying to claim me just 'cause I'm sick."

The sheriff nodded his head for me not to say nothing else and asked Louise if she wanted to go to the hospital or if she wanted to go to jail. She said, "I don't want to go nowhere, and I'm not going to go nowhere! You can't put me no where."

I told him, "Take her to the hospital."

Fighting tooth and toenail, they got her into the ambulance. She begged for a cigarette and begged for a fix. "I would get alright if you would just give me a cigarette," she'd say.

At the hospital, she softened a little and turned to me and said, "Mama, you've done all you can. I want you to know that I love you. I know I haven't been the best daughter lately, but I still love you. I just want to go home."

She looked like death. Her face was white, and she couldn't swallow any food. She had to be fed through her veins, and when she coughed, her chest rattled. The doctors called it the death rattle and said the only hope of her survivin' would be to replace her body.

The doctors were in and out of the room and had announced her dead three different times. It was really hard. I didn't leave her bedside. I stayed there until the last breath left her. She fought it to the last minute. I remembered the words of Berta Mae Nolan, "If you ever do have any children, it don't matter what they get in to, you be there. You be there for them. You have that much love in your soul."

When Louise finally took her last breath, I stood over her body and took her head in my hands. I cried out, "Oh, Lord, not my daughter! Not my dear precious daughter!" I held on to her for a short while, then placed her hands near her sides and pushed her eyelids closed.

I picked up my purse, shook my shoulders, and walked around to the office and told the doctors, "You can pronounce Edna Louise Allen as deceased."

"Are you sure?" The doctor asked. "We've been called three times, and every time we've been wrong."

"I know she's gone this time. I'm her mother."

I finally lost my oldest daughter, Louise. She had one stroke right on top of another. She spent nine weeks in the North Memorial Hospital before she finally passed away. She suffered death, and I was right there with her. The doctors wanted to know if I wanted them to drive me home or call somebody to come and get me. I said, "I've been through this for the last five years, and I would rather just handle this by myself my way."

Sure enough, I come on home and I made it through it, but I want you to know how awful it is for the people that are left behind. How they suffer watching their young waste away on these drugs. It hurts, and it hurts deep. I raised six children, and of the six, four of them got into drugs. I've already lost two, and the others are still into them. I can't talk about it without crying. It causes my heart to hurt me. I've suffered a lot of deaths, and I've suffered a lot of things that was unnecessary on account of the drugs. But I want you to know, mothers and fathers, that my heart goes out to you. The only way to get it behind us is to pray about it.

I thank God I've lived a long life, and I've lived a lot of it by Berta Mae's words: "It doesn't matter what my kids get into, I am always right there waiting for 'em."

I Thank God I was strong enough through it all and that I never got into drugs—not even doctors' drugs—not any kind of drugs. But I haven't been strong by myself. Jesus has been through it with me. All the way through it. He dried my tears when there weren't any tears to be dried. He's led my hand and kept me safe through all the terrifying things I went through.

It always makes me nervous to talk about a death, but this needed to be said, and what happened. Amen.

Chapter Twenty-Four
1994

A doctor at Scenic General Hospital called and asked me to bring him some herbs and minerals. He was treating an AIDS patient, and wanted some help from me because I had been doctoring some of his AIDS patients through him.

While I was waiting for him in the waiting room, this woman come out of the doctors' office cryin' like her little heart would break. She was a little thing with a whiny voice, and I imagine she was about sixty years-old. She was cryin' and cryin', and I put my arm around her and said, "It can't be that bad, honey. It can't be that bad."

She said, "Oh, yes it is—it's worse. I don't have another livin' soul in the world but my son, and they're sending him home to die. You'll see him come through here."

Sure enough, this little man come out into the waiting room and he was skin and bones. He was six foot tall, and he wouldn't have weighed seventy-five pounds. He had AIDS so bad he was wearin' white shorts that went just below the knees and blood was done runnin' out of his rectum down both sides of his legs. They was sendin' him home to die.

Instead of givin' the herbs to the doctor that had ordered them from me, I took them out of my purse and gave them to her. I said, "Honey, you take these herbs and these minerals, and you do what I say. I won't guarantee that it will cure him, but I guarantee it will help him."

She says, "He hasn't had a bit of nothin' to eat in eight months other than baby food!"

At about three o'clock in the afternoon she took him home, and she made the tea like I told her to, and she gave him a dose of the minerals. Long about six o'clock she gets on the phone, and she calls me in her whiny voice. She says, "My son is hungry, what'll I do? He ain't had no food in his stomach now in eight months. Nothin' but baby food!"

"Well, I tell you what I'd do if it were my son. I would go to one of the best stores around and I'd get me one of the biggest, tenderest steaks. I'd get two big steaks—get him one and get you one, too. It won't hurt you either to have something to eat. Bake him a big, nice Irish potato and get some asparagus and put it on his plate. Cook some hot biscuits and feed him."

"Won't it kill him?"

"Well, honey, I wasn't gonna tell you this, but this is the way I feel. If the doctor said he sent him home to die, let him die with a full stomach."

He ate it all, and at about ten o'clock while I was at her place, she came out of his room to tell me, "He's asleep, Lady Nellie. He is asleep."

"Yes, Ma'am, you let him sleep as long as he wants to. Don't try to get him up. Let him sleep."

She said, "Don't let him get up to get his medicine?"

"No, you give him what I told you" and set the doctor's medicine on the shelf.

The next mornin' she called me and said, "It stayed down. Now what'll I feed him?"

"Go and cook him some hot biscuits and gravy and a little fried Irish potato."

I never heard from that woman no more for about six months, and one day here comes this tiny, squeakin' voice. She said, "My son has put on about seventy-five pounds of weight and he's doin' real good, but I am out of herbs and minerals."

I said, "Well, if you'll run over here, I'll give you another six months' supply."

I was giving her the herbs and minerals and things because he was my first AIDS patient and because I loved her. I wanted her to have her son.

"I want you to know," she said, "I ain't got a penny to pay you. I ain't got a nickel! I have spent everything that we had on him!"

I said, "Well, just run by my house and you can pick some up."

"I don't have a car. I sold my car for his doctor bill."

"Well, I'll tell you what I'll do. I'll put it in your mailbox."

I did just that. I took it to her place and put it in the mailbox, and the little thing came to the door and waved at me as I drove off.

I never heard from that woman until five years later. She called and said, "Lady Nellie, my son is feeling better and is back to work. God bless you and thank you for your help."

Chapter Twenty-Five
Modesto

2000-2003

I want to get around to tellin' you the story about my sister Hattie runnin' away from a rest home. When Hattie and her husband, Parker Dodson, left the cotton fields years ago, they settled back in Avinger, Texas, and bought an acre of ground with a little house on it. Parker was a blind man. He drew a blind pension for the family. To earn some extra money for the family, Hattie took in laundry for the little town of Avinger through the week. On a Sunday, why she would go to church and babysit all the children at the little Baptist Church. She did that for years.

When Edna and her husband, Howard Brown, left the cotton fields, they made up their minds they wouldn't pick cotton no more. They bought a little farm about eight miles out in the country from Lindon, and raised chickens, hogs, cows, and big gardens with Tom Watson watermelons that were so big you could put a great big kid inside the rind.

Papa lived with Hattie. He helped cut wood and helped raised the chickens at Hattie's place. We were all workers. We were all poor folks, but we survived. We all knowed to work to survive.

Papa finally passed. That morning he washed his hands and face and went to the eating table, and he told Hattie, "Fix me a Nellie cup of coffee."

That meant the coffee had cream, sugar, and milk in the cup of coffee. She left to go to the kitchen to get the coffee for him, and when she returned he was dead. He had pushed his plate back and laid his head on the table. They said his heart just wore plumb out on him.

Hattie has a big family, nine children I think all together, and an awful lot of grandkids and great-grandkids. But, nobody wanted to take care of her. All you could hear whenever I went back there to Texas to see them, and every time I turned around, "Put Mama in the hospital. Put Mama in the convalescent hospital." Well, I think they put people in old folks' homes to kill them, or so they'll pass away quicker to get rid of them.

Hattie had been there at the rest home three years, and she kept wantin' out. She finally got a hold of me and told me she was wantin' to come to me. Well, I'd seen a vision. I seen these big gates openin' up and lettin' her come free. So, I called her and I said, "Listen, I saw the gates outside the rest home openin' up on a Thursday evening, and there would be nobody watching, and you walkin' out 'em and gettin' away and comin' to me. You'll get out of your wheelchair and walk straight out the back door and through the gates. There would be a friend there waiting on you."

Now, I saw a vision of this a month before it happened.

I got a hold of another friend of ours and said, "Hattie wants out of the rest home. She wants to come and live with me, and this is fine 'cause I'll take care of her."

Sure enough, whenever the day come, Hattie got up out of her wheelchair and left it in the bathroom so it wouldn't be noticeable and walked out the back door, and those gates were wide open. She walked right through the gates and got in my friend's car and my friend taken her straight to the airport. She got on that plane and come to me.

The nurses and kids couldn't find her, and I wouldn't tell them where she was at 'cause they would have come right on out and got her. Some of her kids just throwed the awfullest fit you ever heard in your life because she come to me. Well, we were sisters, and she come to me.

We met Hattie at the airplane and brought her straight home. I got her a wheelchair so she could be comfortable, and she done pretty good while she was here. She got to where she could get out of that chair and walk around the house. We'd go shopping and out to eat and everything, and go here and go there and visit my children. Of course, I sell the Andara

Crystals, and she enjoyed watching me do that. We had a real good time during the three years she was here with me.

She never was a great big woman no how; she always weighed about a hundred pounds. But she come out here and got up to a hundred and forty pounds. She said to me when she was here, "My goodness, I'm fatter than I've ever been in my life, but I feel good."

We talked about things her kids told me. They'd say, "Oh, Mama's senile. She's this, she's that." But the truth of it was, there was that big bunch of kids and 'nare one of them had time for her.

We talked about all the moanin' and groanin' that went on in the rest home, and how they would all gather in the common area in their wheelchairs and cry and beg to go home. Some would sit there and cry and some would laugh about nothing. Some would even call Hattie their sister or their mother, and it made her very nervous and very upset about life. It caused her to have nightmares.

The food was awful, too. There were English peas and she didn't like them. She didn't like the old broccoli either. She said it tasted like wood.

We talked about our mama singing to us while we set in the wagon, traveling to the beautiful Kiamichi Mountains, and telling us about the animals and comforting us. We remembered Mama killing the squirrels and making squirrel dumplings out of them. We remembered camping out and being afraid of the voices we heard coming from the woods. Mama would say, "That's the sound of the coyote."

We talked about the cotton fields and the good old days of watching the beautiful red sunset over the white fields of cotton. We remembered the critical days at the orphanage and how happy we was when Papa came.

Me and Hattie thought of all the old days and how we made it through it together. Sometimes we would be talking to each other about the past and we would be left in tears. Others times we would bust a gut laughing 'til we almost lost our breath and passed out on the floor from laughter. It wouldn't have been so bad if we would have passed out, for we would have been together. We are true sisters.

After three years, everyday or two, Hattie would say, "I'm gonna die, and I don't want to die in California! I want to go home to die."

I was beggin' with tears in my eyes, "Honey, I'll take care of you if you'll just stay with me. I've got this big house here and I can take care of you."

"Well, I know I'm gonna die, and I don't want to die in California 'cause it's too much trouble," she'd say.

She was wantin' to go back and see the kids—I know what she was wantin' to do. And I would tell her, "Hattie, honey—you know if you go back there they're gonna put you right back there in that old rest home. If not in that one, then another one."

"No, they won't this time. They miss me so bad they won't put me back in a rest home."

I put her on an airplane and sent her home, and I want you to know she hadn't been back home six weeks and they done stuck her back in that old rest home. She's been there ever since. She got blue for the kids, but the kids didn't get blue for her, I'll tell you for sure.

If it was left up to me, she'd be right here in California with me. Of course, it wasn't left up to me. I miss that woman. That's my oldest sister, Hattie Dodson. She run away from the convalescent hospital in Texas and come to me. There wasn't a day that went by that me and her didn't have a little prayer and praise God for the time we had together. Not one.

God bless my sister Hattie, and God bless my little sister Edna. We've made all the depressions, we've buried our young, and us three girls are all still alive and still know our own name. It hasn't been an easy life, but it's been a life.

Chapter Twenty-Six
Modesto

2003-present

This chapter is about Lady Nellie Thompson and Billy Chief Smith. It's concerning a love story. I don't know how it happened hardly, but it did happen, and it's still happenin'. This story started four years ago, February the 21st.

I woke up from a dead sleep to some of the sweetest music I had ever heard. It was an Indian love song. I couldn't figure out where in the world I was or what in the world was happening or where the music was coming from. I got up and tip-toed into the living room to see if the television was still on. It wasn't. I went back, and I sat down on the edge of the bed. I moved the curtain a little bit and here was a young man sitting out in front of my window and, mind you, it was cold, misty, and rainy—singing and playing his guitar. His hair was all strung down over his face and come down on his chest. He was soaking wet.

I went to the door and asked, "What in the world do you mean by being out in that rain?"

He looked up and said, "Well, I was trying to wake you up to wish you happy birthday. I guess you know I know how old you are, but that's okay, I'm waking you up anyhow."

I offered him a cup of coffee, but he wouldn't come in the house 'cause he said he was too wet and messy. He said, "I'd hug you, but honest to God, I don't want to get you wet and make you sick." I was standing in the doorway in my pink cotton gown, and he was playing and singing to me. It was a real kind, warm, gentle song.

The next day he came, and he was all smooth shaved and his hair was back in a ponytail, and he said, "How are you doing this morning, young lady?"

"All right," I told him.

"Do you know I've been chasing you around about a year, just to say hello?"

I've always been a busy woman minding my own business and didn't notice. I have all my family and grandkids, and as far as I was concerned I was making a good living and was happy with what I had. My husband had been dead for twenty-five years, and there hadn't been a sign of a man in my life during these years. I didn't want one. I didn't want one to have to wait on and put up with. I didn't want no man in my life.

When he got ready to leave, he wanted a big hug and a kiss. He rolled me up in his arms and held me close to his chest. I hug people from all over the world that come and see me so I didn't think anything about it.

That spring, he brought me a little angel rag doll. It was a beautiful day, and the roses and honeysuckle vines were all in bloom and let off a beautiful fragrance. It smelled like fresh roses inside the gate and then as you got closer to the house the honeysuckle vines taken over and let off a sweet fragrance.

Chief sat and visited with me for about an hour, and he asked me if I would go with him. I had to have time to think that one over, I'll tell you for sure—'cause here I am, eighty-five years old, and he's fifty. There was such a difference in our ages until I couldn't believe it. I didn't want to believe it, I guess.

When he got ready to leave he hugged and kissed me again, and this time it was kind of a strange hug—a little bit more than friendship. It was a real, good tender-loving hug.

He always made it up here once or twice a month. I couldn't understand why he and my son were such good friends, but I found out later it wasn't my son that he was interested in. It was me! We've had a lot of good laughs and have gone many places. We go out to dinner once or twice a week together, and this goes on for about three years.

About a year ago, he got so sick he could hardly get out of the chair. He said, "I've got walking pneumonia, and the doctor doesn't know what to do for me. He's done everything he knows to do."

"Oh, well, fiddle. Let me make you some tea and get you past it."

While he was out there visiting with my son and the other people in the yard, I went in and made him a gallon of tea and got him some minerals and started him on it.

He stayed two or three days there with my son David. He would come back every day and visit a little bit with me. He's just kind of a shy guy. He don't have much to say to nobody. He hopes everybody understands him, I guess. He asked me again, "Nellie, would you go with me?"

"Oh, fiddle, no," I told him.

"Why not?"

"Don't you know there's so much difference in our ages?"

"Would you just let me worry about that? I happen to know you're the best cook in the country."

"Well, lah-di-dah."

We started going together, speaking together at least, and stealing a hug here and there. Then one day I came down with the West Nile virus. I was so sick and had been to the hospital three times before they found out what was wrong with me. I was in there eight days, and sure enough, Chief came to see me.

I told him I would be home in the morning, and well, here was Chief the next morning in front of my house. He opened the car door and put his arms around me and practically carried me to the bed. He always smelled clean and fresh, and I loved being cuddled. He covered me up and wanted to know if I wanted something to eat.

"You can go when you're ready. I can make it from here on."

"I'm not going anywhere," he said. "I am going to nurse you back to health. I can't afford to lose you now."

He never left my side long enough to do anything but get us some food. He washed my clothes, kept my house, cooked my food, and nursed me back to health. He stayed right there and did everything he could to make me content and to see that I got back to health. He said, "Honey, the minute I know you're able to take care of yourself, I will get me a job and go back to work and make a living. I've never loved somebody so much in my entire life. You've taught me more about love than I thought I would ever learn."

The kids got to where they couldn't stand him because I thought so much of him. My daughter Leona was awful fussy about him, always asking where he was going and what he was doing. It didn't make a difference to me where he went because he was taking care of me.

I had made up my mind that there was too much difference in our ages, but when we were together we would never believe it. We laughed, we talked, we visited, and we had a good time. But, I felt he could find someone his own age and there was no need to go on with it.

Then one day, I looked out my front window, and I received a great message. I could see two red tail hawks sittin' in the very top of a great big walnut tree across the street from me over at my son George's house. They weren't circling yet. Usually when I have company, they show up two or three at a time and soar in wide circles above my house to give me a great blessing for my company. I had a feeling that it wouldn't be long before company was a comin'.

Then, when the hawks started circling above my rooftop, and the flowers in my yard were beautiful and full of color, I looked out the window and here come Chief. He was walking in almost a run up to my front door, and the tears were just rollin' down his face. He opened the door, and I had done got up and started to the door, and we met each other in the middle of the floor, and we both cried like two babies.

"I can't let you go. I love you too much," he said. "I will always love you."

"Yeah, well, look at our ages."

"Let me worry about that. You're the best woman, and you've showed me nothing but kindness since I've known you. Besides, you saved my life when I had that walking pneumonia, and I don't intend to give up now."

Sure enough, we got to where we were going together real steady and went out to eat and went on Sunday drives.

"I've asked you to marry me twice now, Nellie. Will you marry me?"

"I can't because all the finances I have coming in will stop."

"I know I can make us a living, and I'm not going to let go."

He always calls me nearly twice a day, and a lot of times when he leaves he gets out to the gate, then turns around and comes and hugs and kisses me again. We are that close to each other.

I need his love and I know it. I don't know how I had lived that long without love, all on my own. Whenever I see him, it brings a smile to my face and happiness to my heart. I will always be right here waiting for him, if it's the Lord's will.

I'm going to close my little love story about Chief. There wouldn't be anything that would make me happier this day than to see that man walk through the gate. I know he feels the same way.

Chapter Twenty-Seven
2009

My grandfather started my life out. He held me up to the Great White Father, Jesus, and declared me a princess. He declared that I would live a long life and have many tests and trials before the end of time.

I'm ninety years-old now, and I have made it with many blessings along the way. Being an Indian princess hasn't been easy, you know. But, I've tried to fulfill the Choctaw Tribe's wishes by serving God.

It's really important for us older folks to share our lives with the young so they will gain knowledge about life, too. Just as I learned from my ancestors, I would love for the young to learn from me. I love my tribe. I love the Indian culture. I love my Indian mother, and I am grateful to the Indian chiefs that walked in front of us and led the way. Pushmataha was the beginning of a great culture. He was a smart and intelligent man, and he led the tribe into wealth and happiness. He brought two races together, the White and the Indians, to where they could live on this earth in peace together.

God made room for each and everyone of us.

At the age of eighty-eight years old, I started going to school to learn to read and write. I can now read a letter. It's never too late to get an education. As long as there is breath, there is hope.

Sixty years I've been here in Modesto and, well, I guess I'll die in Modesto. Unless I get a wild hair to go to Hawaii or Oklahoma or somewhere else to pass out, I'll be right here in Modesto.

I'd just like to tell the world, don't give up on God. You might think that He's give up on you, but He's always right there with a helping hand. All you've got to do is ask for it. That's the sum of my story.

Epilogue

Before meeting Nellie Thompson, I never expected to leave my career in childhood education to teach an eighty-eight-year-old woman to read and write, then plunge into writing her life story and, for the first time, come to really understand the true value of literacy. As a teacher of children, I of course had a sense of the importance of being able to read and write, but in my experience with this extraordinary woman, I have discovered the magic it is to be able to unlock and capture the mind of an individual.

After learning to read and discovering a world that had been previously closed to her, Nellie felt compelled to read all that she had missed in her life. Even as an illiterate woman, she had sensed the importance of learning to read and write, and as you have seen, that sense drove her to leave a fairly secure world to take her children to Modesto, a place she believed held the key to their future success and happiness—an education. "Everybody always appears to me when they have a good education, that they have everything," she would frequently tell me.

For eighteen months she's read and read and read, and I've listened and written. It's been two women living the power of reading and writing. She started at eighty-eight. I started at thirty-one. She's been an adult for a long time; I'm catching up, and now we're dear friends.

I've thought a lot about what Lady Nellie has said—how educated people appear to have everything—and I'm reminded of a sweet memory.

I followed her one Tuesday, a few weeks after we first met, through a hallway that led to the rear of her home. Three carpenters were framing up the walls for a spare bedroom.

"Drive the nails in at 45 degrees," she told one of the workers as her slippers slowly shuffled across the dusty floor. "A little slant in the nail will make it more secure.

"And if you'll soak the ends of the nails in a little oil or beeswax, it will make them go into the dried-out wood without bendin'.

The room grew silent. Then I heard a low voice from the corner.

"She keeps us in line," one worker said, smiling.

I followed her back to the living room and watched her plop down in her leather rocking chair. I sat next to her and put my hand on her knee. "You're smart, Lady Nellie. You're a real smart woman."

"Oh, no," she said, waving her hand toward the ground, "that's just something I remember Papa teachin' me when I was a little girl."

A few weeks later, our reading lessons ended as we began capturing her life story on tape. "I can always go back and pick up my schooling, even at my age," she told me. "Besides, as bad as I want to learn to read and write, can you imagine me furnishin' other people reading?"

I smiled at the thought and knew she had a lot to share with the world.

As time moved forward, I listened to her stories and worked on transcribing our conversations. When I called her on the phone and told her I had actually completed the transcription, she poured her heart out to me.

"The truth is—this is the first time in history some of these stories have ever been told. I thank God for lettin' me have the opportunity and strength, which it hurts still yet, to mention some of these things."

"You're a true survivor, Lady Nellie, and you're still here to tell your story!"

"I sure am. I'm still here to tell my story and thank God. To put this all on paper and to bring out all the things that have happened during my life has been real hard on me; but it's been healing. I know it will bring tears, but tears are worth having.

"As long as there is breath in my body, I hope and pray to God I can serve Him well, as God has served me. He has been with me all these years—through all these trials.

"I want people to know the very first thing you should do in life is find God, and He will see you through the worst and bless you through the best. Before my children were old enough to talk, I would teach them, 'Jesus watches over us, Jesus is our way of life, Jesus owns the ground and heaven above, and we're in between.'

"I cling to Christ but honor and respect all walks of life that include God."

I sat next to her and smiled at her wisdom.

"Lady Nellie, thanks for sharing your heart with me, and with the world. You're one educated woman."

About the Authors

Nellie M. Thompson lives in Modesto, California, where she is surrounded by family and friends that love her. She enjoys the simple pleasures of life and praises God for each new day.

Wendy Ann Cope lives in Orem, Utah. She enjoys spending time outdoors and believes with God, nothing is impossible

Made in the USA
Middletown, DE
29 November 2021